AF606908

ENDORSEMENTS

Perris Jones is the epitome of a guy you want to be in the foxhole with. Adversity seems to be underneath his feet at all times.

—Mike Hollins
University of Virginia Football '24

I've had the privilege of watching Perris Jones grow not just as a football player, but as a man of uncommon character and courage. Perris faced adversity with humility, resilience, and quiet strength, earning the respect of teammates, coaches, and this entire community. His book reflects the same honesty and depth we saw in him every day. He was clear-eyed about hardship, yet anchored in hope and purpose. This is the voice of a leader who understands that true impact isn't measured in yards gained, but in lives influenced.

—Dr. Carla Williams
Director of Athletics, University of Virginia

Perris Jones is one of the most resilient and grounded young men I've had the privilege to know. His integrity, work ethic, and unwavering spirit in the face of adversity speak volumes about the kind of leader and human being he is.

—Dr. Pat Ivey
Senior Associate Athletic Director of
Health and Performance, University of Louisville

There are many hard workers in this world. I have yet to meet one who can match the level of resiliency and integrity that Perris Jones carries—every single day.

—Joshua Rawlings, BA
University of Virginia Football '24

Perris Jones is an inspiration to us all. He has earned a lifetime of doing the ordinary—and the extraordinary—extraordinarily well. He has walked the talk. When many of us step back from the mountain in front of us, Perris has smiled and leaned into the climb. Over years of working with elite-level people and athletes, his story is rare and precious in defining the "because of" mindset that any of us can embrace our setbacks and suffering as the fuel to pursue our best selves.

—Jason Freeman, PhD
Licensed Clinical and Sport Psychologist, University of Virginia School of Medicine

Perris is one of the toughest and most competitive players I have been lucky to coach. He played with a contagious smile, but worked with a chip on his shoulder. He has never wavered from his resilient mindset. Perris is an amazing person, and I cannot wait to see what he accomplishes.

—Matt John
Quarterback Coach, Utah State University

Perris Jones is uncommon; truly a rare man with an infectious attitude, supreme leadership, and unmatched toughness. When he speaks, all should listen.

—Nate Pototschnik, "Blackjack"
Associate Director Strength and Conditioning Football,
Brigham Young University

Perris is an exceptional young man with an amazing story to tell. Life is about accepting and growing from the challenges that come our way. Perris's ability to navigate and persevere through the unique obstacles he has already faced in his short life should motivate all of us. It will be an honor to read Perris Jones's story as he explains how he has turned tragic moments into a truly inspirational life.

—Josh Heird
Athletic Director, University of Louisville

It is my true honor to recommend Ashes to Endzone. I have known Perris ever since he was under my care, and his story is one of remarkable grace, resilience, and grit. In this remarkable story, Perris shares how he faced paralysis and the decision to leave the game he had loved since he was a kid. I can only imagine the strength it has taken to recover and the inspirational decision to pursue a doctorate at the institution that treated him. I have been fortunate to play a small part in what God is doing in his life and look forward to the impact he will undoubtedly have through this book.

—Max Boakye
Neurosurgeon, University of Louisville

ASHES TO ENDZONE

THE FIGHT FOR IDENTITY, FAITH, AND A FUTURE BIGGER THAN THE GAME

ASHES TO ENDZONE

THE FIGHT FOR IDENTITY, FAITH, AND A FUTURE BIGGER THAN THE GAME

Perris Jones

Printed in the United States of America
Published by Igniting Souls
PO Box 43, Powell, OH 43065
IgnitingSouls.com

LCCN: 2026900626
Paperback ISBN: 978-1-63680-612-9
Hardback ISBN: 978-1-63680-613-6
eBook ISBN: 978-1-63680-614-3

Available in paperback, hardcover, e-book, and audiobook.

CONTENTS

FOREWORD

I first met Perris Jones in July 2024, and within minutes of hearing his story, I knew I was in the presence of something extraordinary. What he shared wasn't just a recounting of events; it was a journey of the soul. One moment, I was laughing at his humor and humility; the next, I was angry at the injustice he endured. Then came the quiet moments that brought tears, and finally, the overwhelming sense of hope that only comes when you witness true resilience in action.

When he finished, I looked at him and said, "Perris, you can speak on any stage, to any audience, anywhere in the world. The world needs to hear your story." And I meant every word. At the time, I had just founded Character First Athletics, an organization devoted to helping student-athletes anchor their success in integrity, purpose, and faith. I knew immediately that Perris's story would become one of our very first initiatives—a living example of what it means to lead with character, no matter the cost.

Every time I hear or read it, his story moves me all over again. His words don't just inspire; they convict, reminding us that faith is revealed in struggle, not proven in comfort. Perris embodies the kind of strength that can't be taught in a classroom or measured on a scoreboard.

Though decades apart in age, I can say with sincerity: Perris Jones is my friend, and I look up to him. In his life, I see the reflection of the Christian virtues we all strive toward—faith that endures, love that forgives, peace that defies understanding, kindness that softens hearts, and joy that persists even in pain. His light shines all the brighter because it was born in darkness.

My prayer is that, as you turn these pages, you will feel what I felt that first day—moved, challenged, and inspired to believe that no matter where you come from or what you've faced, your story still matters.

Jonathan Cotten
Founder, Character First Athletics
CEO, Easy Step Enterprises dba The Good Feet Store

PRELUDE

My name is Perris Jones, and this is my story.

This isn't just a book about football. It's not just about a spinal cord injury or a life turned upside down in one brutal, irreversible moment. It's about everything that happens *after.*

After the crowd goes silent.

After the field clears.

After the lights dim and you're left alone with a future that no longer looks anything like the one you'd built in your head since you were a child.

But this isn't simply a story about surviving trauma.

It's about staring down the wreckage and refusing to let it define the rest of your life.

It's about learning how to breathe when tomorrow's mystery grips your lungs.

It's about learning to *see* again—not with your eyes, but with the kind of vision that only reveals itself when the world you once knew vanishes beneath you.

Because when the body breaks, something else begins to form in its place. A different kind of strength. Strength not measured by speed or weight or yards gained—but by the depth of your soul, and your willingness to fight for something bigger than yourself.

This story begins in the silence. In the paralyzing stillness after impact, when you're lying on your back, unable to move, unsure if you ever will again, when the sky above feels endless, but your body feels like a prison. When your loved ones form a circle around you and all you can see are their faces twisted in worry, but you can't even lift your head to reassure them that you're okay, because you're not sure that you are.

In those moments, the pain isn't what crushes you. It's the *not knowing*. The terrifying possibility that life, as you know it, ends. Leaving you with nothing but questions: Who are you now? Without everything you had previously used to define yourself? What do you hold onto when everything you've built feels like it's slipping through your fingers?

But this book is not about despair. It's about *what comes next*. It's about the shift that happens when you stop asking, "Why me?" (a question that will never have a satisfying answer), and start asking the question that actually matters: *"What now?"*

You see, adversity doesn't simply knock you down, nor does it strip you bare. It *demands* that you rise again, and rise differently. Not with the same stride, or the same plans, but with something more profound. It teaches you to rebuild from the inside out. Brick by painful, stubborn brick. It invites you to dig into the parts of yourself that no crowd ever cheers for. The grit. The grace. The faith. The stillness. The courage to keep moving forward when every logical part of you is screaming to give up.

If you're reading this, and you're facing your own version of that moment—the silent stadium, the shattered dream, the diagnosis, the phone call in the middle of the night—then know this: I wrote this book for *you*.

Not to tell you life is fair. Because it isn't. Life will take things from you without apology. People will move on while you're still learning how to sit up in bed. And that truth is brutal.

I'm here to tell you that even when everything seems lost, when the world feels unrecognizable, when hope feels out of reach, there *is* still a way forward. And sometimes, what waits on the other side of that fire is greater than anything you could've ever drawn up for yourself. Because when life tears away everything, it gives you the rarest opportunity: to build something true. Something whole. Something *new*.[IP]

I'm not here to sell you a lie or to sugarcoat suffering. And I won't tell you it's easy. Because it's not. Some days, it will feel like you're trying to walk through fire barefoot. But sometimes, in life, you have to go through the fire, the compression, the consistent pressure, to uncover the diamond hidden in the depths of your being.

INTRODUCTION

"Get up, Perris."

That was the first thought to echo in my mind after the impact. It was sharp, desperate, almost involuntary. A reflex. The kind of instinct forged by years of playing this game, of getting hit and rising without hesitation.

It was late in the third quarter, and our team was finally gaining momentum. The energy on the sideline had shifted, the crowd beginning to rise with every first down. We had our opponents on their heels, and everyone in the stadium could feel it. The call came in: *"Trips Right Rikers."*

It was a play I knew by heart, and a staple in our offense. I'd probably run it a thousand times in practice, maybe more. It was muscle memory at this point. Still, as I jogged up to the line, I did what I always did: surveyed the defense. Calm, methodical.

There was a tag on the play. If the numbers were better backside, meaning that the offense would have more blockers than defenders, the quarterback would check to a smoke screen. If not, it was a designed flair to me in the flat. As I looked across the line, I saw man coverage. The advantage was ours, and the ball was coming my way.

The snap came. I exploded out of my stance, attempting to gain leverage on the defender responsible for guarding me, eyes, shoulders, and hips facing toward the sideline, took three hard steps, then pivoted in preparation for the pass. The ball was already in the air, spinning tightly, almost suspended in time. I reached out, caught it cleanly, and turned to calculate my next move.

The outside defender overcommitted, meaning he overplayed his position to my outside, clearing the inside lane. I recognized it instantly, planting my right foot into the ground, I cut upfield, slipping inside my blocker. A lane was open just long enough for me to see it. Just long enough for two defenders to collapse on me.

I braced myself like I had so many times before. Shoulders tight, core locked, biting down on my mouthpiece like I was attempting to tear a rough piece of licorice, ready to take the hit and drive through. I expected a thud, a roll, followed by a teammate's outstretched hand pulling me to my feet, and the jog back to the huddle. But that's not what happened. Two Louisville defenders collided with me simultaneously, and everything went blank.

I didn't feel the ground meet my back. I didn't feel pain. I felt no tingling, typical of a stinger, which I presumed this to be, no slight tingling in the extremities that fades as time goes on. I didn't feel the slight breeze sneaking between the slits in the stadium, the vibration of the crowd noise, or the cold drip of sweat beneath the pads down my back. I didn't feel anything. All I felt was an increasing sense of fear building inside of me, like a roller coaster climbing to its drop point.

It was as if my body had disappeared beneath me, like I had become a ghost in my own skin. The lights above blurred into a blinding halo, white and unrelenting, burning into my vision. The roar of the stadium dimmed into silence, as if I had been plunged underwater.

And then came the panic. I tried to move. Nothing.

Get up, Perris.

Still nothing. I repeated the thought like a prayer, trying to will myself into motion. My brain fired commands that my body had always responded to, but in this moment, my limbs lay still, detached and foreign. My body had betrayed me for the first time in my life.

And then the thoughts rushed in like a flood:

Am I paralyzed?

Will I ever walk again?

What happens now?

Why now? Why me?

What am I going to do?

How will I take care of my family?

Each question hit harder than the tackle itself. In that moment, lying on the field surrounded by flashing lights and unfamiliar silence, I wasn't an athlete. I wasn't a starter, a playmaker, a teammate. I was a broken body with a racing mind, trying to understand what had just been taken from me.

The Louisville trainers got to me first. I could see the concern on their faces as they hovered above me. Typically, in football, if the other trainers come to you, you know it's bad. It's customary for your team's trainers to come to you, no matter where you are on the field. However, this instance was different. Their lips were moving, but their words were distant echoes, muted by the chaos in my head. I saw hands on my helmet, fingers motioning in front of my eyes. Still, I couldn't move, I couldn't feel anything. Not even a twitch.

It was as if time slowed to a crawl. Every second felt like an eternity, every breath a countdown to some unspoken fate. In my mind, the worst-case scenario played on a cruel, endless loop. I imagined myself never walking again. Trapped in a wheelchair, helpless, watching as the muscles I had built with years of discipline and sacrifice wasted away day by day. The strong, sculpted frame I had once taken pride in would slowly vanish, and with it, the identity I had poured my soul into.

Who would want to spend their life with someone who couldn't even stand on their own? What kind of partner would I be, or rather, what kind of burden? Would I ever hold a child of my own, feel them run into my arms, teach them to walk, or play catch? Those dreams, once so vivid, now flickered in the haze of uncertainty. If I was paralyzed, I would have to live in a body that no longer felt like mine. I would be forced to find peace in a future I hadn't chosen.

As they wheeled me off the field, the stadium roared. The crowd's cheers swelled behind me, a sound meant to lift my spirits, but in that moment, they only amplified the fear inside. And yet, somewhere in that noise, I found enough courage to ask the question that had already swallowed me whole. I turned to Ashley Murray, our trainer, my voice trembling, and asked, "Am I paralyzed?"

What had started as just another football play unfolded into something far more profound. That was the moment everything changed. The field no longer felt like a stage, but a battlefield, and I was no longer an athlete. I was a survivor in the making. As the stretcher wheeled me off the turf I had bled my entire life for, the lights above blurring into streaks, I wasn't just leaving the game. I was entering the hardest, most significant chapter of my life.

1

THE PLACE THAT RAISED ME

I was born on October 17, 1998, in Port Charlotte, Florida, but my story took its first real breath in the soul of Arcadia. *'Cadi Boyz, stand up!* To most, Arcadia is just a speck on the map, a place you might pass through without noticing. But to me? Arcadia was *everything*. Tucked inland between cow pastures and orange groves, it wasn't just where I lived; it was who I was.

I used to joke that Arcadia was an "all-inclusive resort." Not because it was luxurious (far from it), but because it had everything we needed: family, food, faith, and a whole lot of fight. For many of us, it was the beginning, middle, and end of our world. You were born there, went to school there, spent your summers there, and if you weren't careful, you'd die on the same porch you grew up watching your uncles sip their 40s. To this day, I can still name the old heads who never left those porches, faces weathered like the chipped paint beneath them. Time moved, but most folks didn't. Arcadia was a cycle. A rhythm. A closed loop with no easy way out.

If you grew up there, you didn't just live in a neighborhood, you *survived* in it. Our streets didn't have names that meant anything to the outside world, but to us, they were stadiums, battlegrounds, and sacred ground. We didn't need cleats; we had calloused feet, sun-baked and born for the grind. We ran routes through grass scarred by what most would consider poverty, between project buildings that leaned like tired shoulders. The sidelines weren't chalk; littered, broken Heineken bottles, crushed Budweisers, and forgotten glass shimmering like landmines under weeds marked the boundaries. Every cut, every sprint, was a gamble. But we moved like pain was part of the plan.

Basketball lived wherever we breathed; bent rims, rusted poles, milk or Rubbermaid bins flipped and baptized into purpose. Courts were concrete dreams, stitched together with sweat, scuffed shoes, and whatever we had left in our tanks.

Home wasn't a picket-fenced house. Home was my grandparents' place with floors that groaned like the elders when you walked on them, a garage door rusted shut since before I could remember, and a back den with no A/C where I fought off the Florida heat with a box fan and pure willpower. When I wasn't there, I was with my mom, and where we lay our heads depended on who she was with. Sometimes it was a boyfriend's place. Sometimes, a room at the Best Western, where roaches and other insects scurried in dark corners. Sometimes, it was a trap house floor with a mattress on one side, a broken coffee table on the other, and white powder scattered in random places. Childhood didn't always feel like childhood; it felt like survival with a side of make-believe. Most days, we lived in Section 8 housing, paint peeling from the walls faster than the landlords could pretend to care.

Arcadia had its own map: Harlem Heights, the Subdivision, Park Place, and the White Section across the tracks. Each one with its own rhythm, but all of us were stitched together by struggle, heat, and a sense of community that raised you even when your parents couldn't.

Discipline wasn't a family thing; it was a neighborhood thing. You could catch a hug at one house and a whooping at the next, and both came from love. Nobody needed an invite, nobody needed permission. Doors stayed open. You just walked in, grabbed a plate, or got corrected, depending on what you needed the most at that moment.

And Sundays? Sundays were sacred. Church started at seven a.m. sharp—pressed shirts, starched slacks, and no excuses. The pews groaned from either the weight of sweat or the presence of the Holy Spirit, depending on who you asked. Auntie caught the Ghost like clockwork, falling out in the third row, while the preacher baptized us with his words like he was trying to drown every demon passed down through the bloodlines. But the real resurrection happened after service: fried chicken that cracked loud as thunder, mac-and-cheese with that thick, perfectly crusted cheese on top, candied yams sticky with love, and sweet tea cold enough to forgive sins. That was my communion.

That was home.

We didn't have much, but we had each other. We had imagination, resilience, and just enough joy to stretch into something that felt like freedom. Every dusty lot was our sold-out football stadium. Every cracked court, a roaring arena. We played for pride, for validation, for the slim chance that the right person might be watching, even if nobody ever was.

And when we weren't hooping or running routes, we were playing manhunt like it was basic training, ducking behind cars, crawling under porches, sprinting barefoot through alleyways with hearts pounding and lungs on fire. We mapped the world one block at a time, piece by piece. We jacked hot links and candy from the convenience store on South Lee Ave, right next to Grandma Mia's house, and hit up the candy lady selling *freezers* and pickled eggs out of her living room. No menus necessary, every item she had was a notorious favorite in the neighborhood.

Haircuts happened on porches. No mirrors, no appointments. Just sit down, hold still, and listen to the grown folks cuss and lie and pass on whatever game they had left. Cookouts were sacred ceremonies. Somebody always had a grill going. Ribs, cornbread, seafood boils, grandpas and uncles flipping chicken religiously as if they were handling the nation's only food supply. And maybe they were: a nation of us, hungry for more than food. We had an undying hunger for belonging, for community.

And when the sun dropped behind the trees, and those street lights flickered on? That was the bell. That was Mama's first and last warning. If you weren't inside by then, expect a switch, a belt, a shoe, or whatever Ma grabbed on instinct. Not out of cruelty, but out of fear. Out of love. Out of the desperate, whispered hope that you'd make it home, *one more night*.

Then came Friday nights. The whole town seemed to pause, even time held its breath. Arcadia's heartbeat wouldn't just pulse; it would thunder beneath the glow of stadium lights. The bleachers would groan with the weight of generations, shoulder to shoulder, where voices would rise like waves. Whether it was the field or the court, those were our sanctuaries. Our battlegrounds. That's where every dream we had took shape, sweat-slicked, adrenaline-fed, and roaring with possibility.

HARDEE VS. DESOTO

The biggest football game of the year. No, the biggest event of the year. In Arcadia, Florida, this wasn't a rivalry. This was tradition. Culture. A clash of identity. The moment fall came alive.

As the sun began to set, the town became consumed with darkness, lit up by the halo-like glow of the Friday night lights. The whole town stood still, and nothing else mattered but the action taking place beneath the glow of fluorescent stadium lights. Businesses shut down early. Parents picked their kids up on time. Traffic thickened around the school by late afternoon. The buzz built up throughout the week, culminating in one singular occasion, unifying a whole town behind one common goal, one common belief: A Bulldog W, a DeSoto W.

And as the day approached, so did the questions. They were rapid-fire, relentless, and trivial, yet critical. *What will I wear? Who's going to be there? When am I getting my haircut?*

The excitement wrapped itself around my seven-year-old self like a vice, squeezing out more of my sleep with every passing day. Every night, I'd toss and turn, visions of the field lights, screaming crowds flashing behind my eyelids.

Thursday finally rolled around, and aspects of the day began to fall into place. Laid out on the bed like an altar to swag was the fit: a fresh pair of Jordan 4s, clean, crisp, and untouched, paired with dark jeans and a blue-and-silver polo that perfectly matched DeSoto's school colors. Dilemma one: solved.

I'd been pestering my mom all week about the haircut; nothing could go right without the cut. It was a sacred ritual. Finally, she came through.

"Haircut's at five p.m. Friday." Just in time. We were cooking now.

Thursday morning felt like Christmas, maybe better. I walked into Memorial Elementary School with a confidence that floated about three inches off the ground. And there she was: Fantaja Ousley, a.k.a. Fancy, the prettiest girl in school, standing by the cafeteria doors like a scene out of a movie.

I approached her with all the smoothness a second grader could muster, trying to play it cool while my heart thumped against my ribcage so hard I swear it was visible through the red Harlem Globetrotters T-shirt I wore.

"You going to the game tomorrow night?" She smiled. "Of course." Boom. Just like that, the stars aligned.

Now, all the boxes were checked, and the ingredients for a once-in-a-lifetime experience set: The fit. Check. The cut. Scheduled. The girl. Confirmed.

The night before the game, sleep was a ghost I kept chasing but could never catch. My body lay still, but on the inside, chaos reigned. My thoughts ran endless wind sprints. The mattress felt like it had springs made of nerves, each toss and turn ricocheting adrenaline through my limbs. I stared at the ceiling until it blurred into shapes I swore were moving, replaying every step, every factor, every possibility of tomorrow like a song or phrase that plays on an infinite loop in your brain. The quiet of the room felt loud, the dark felt alive. Eventually, I stopped pretending. Sleep wouldn't be coming, not tonight. So I lay there, eyes wide open, waiting for the morning light to find me, ready or not.

FRIDAY MORNING. GAME DAY.

The alarm buzzed, and I sprang out of bed. I dressed for school, watching the clock as every minute crawled by slower than the last. The clock hands seemed stuck in place, teasing me.

The day of the game also moved in slow motion. Each class dragged on like my feet through wet cement, every tick of the clock loud enough to echo through my skull. I sat at my desk, bouncing my leg under the table, fingers twitching, mind miles away from the lesson on the board. The teacher's voice sounded like it was underwater, and every time I dared to glance at the clock, only a minute had passed, if that.

At lunch, my tray might as well have been empty. My appetite was gone, replaced by an anxious energy that turned the cafeteria into a pressure cooker. Conversations buzzed around me. Friends laughed, joked, and talked trash about the other team, but all I could hear was the drumbeat of my heartbeat, steady and growing louder by the hour.

Recess or free period was worse. Everyone else scattered across the field or the hallway like it was just another day. But for me, it wasn't. This day was different. It was bigger. I stood on the edge of everything, pacing like a caged dog, glancing up at the sky and imagining the lights that would be on in just a few hours.

And then (finally!) that last bell. I exploded from my seat, barely hearing the teacher's dismissal, barely aware of my own footsteps as I bolted through the hallways and out the doors like they were the gates of a prison. The sun hit my face like a spotlight, and I could finally breathe. Next stop: the barbershop. My ritual. My transformation. Sitting in that chair, watching hair fall away like dead weight, I felt myself becoming who I needed to be. Not just a student anymore. Not a kid. I felt like HIM.

"One guard. Even all around. Line me up." Simple. Clean. Iconic. The kind of cut that turned heads.

We rushed home. I showered, changed, laced up the Jordans, and we left the house, fashionably late, of course. This wasn't the kind of entrance you made early. No, you let the crowd build, and then you arrived, so all eyes could find you.

We pulled up to the school, and it was already chaos. The parking lot was full, packed so tightly you'd think a concert was happening. We parked across the street and walked. And with every step closer to the stadium, my excitement climbed.

I could already hear it: The drums from the marching band, pulsing in rhythm. The roar of the crowd after every big play. The smell of hot dogs, burgers, and kettle corn drifted across the parking lot like a siren song.

By the time I got through the gates, it was everything I dreamed it would be and more. I found my crew. I found Fancy. We laughed, joked, and tossed a football around in the grass behind the stadium like our own little scrimmage before joining the crowd in the stands.

And then I saw them. My cousins, Shed and Shay, in full pads under the stadium lights, commanding the field like warriors. They weren't just players, they were stars. The crowd chanted their names. Every time one of them broke a tackle or made a big hit, I swelled with pride. One day, I thought, *that'll be me.* Wearing that blue and silver. Under these same lights. On this same field.

After the final whistle blew, the night was far from over. In Arcadia, post-game tradition meant one thing: McDonald's. The parking lot came alive when we pulled in. Car doors open, music blasting, headlights bouncing off chrome rims. The inside was buzzing, crowded with classmates, cousins, neighbors, and teachers. Everyone who mattered. It was loud. It was chaotic. It was perfect.

I soaked it all in: friends laughing, music playing, kids reenacting plays from the game in the parking lot, adults catching up on hometown gossip. I remember thinking, *if this is what the rest of my life looks like, it would be everything I could ever hope for.*

Stay in Arcadia. Go to DeSoto High School. Play for the Bulldogs. Get a job at McDonald's. Kick it with my people every Friday night. Simple. Familiar. Fulfilling. Because those nights, under the glow of stadium lights and golden arches, surrounded by everything I loved, I didn't need anything else.

Perris at 7, DCYFL Bulldogs

It wasn't just about the game. It was about pride. It was about family. It was about belonging. I didn't know then how much bigger life could get, or how much pain it might take to realize it, and truthfully, neither did I care.

SHAPED BY COMMUNITY

Arcadia was gritty. Beautiful in its own raw, unpolished way. It taught me that life wouldn't hand you anything, but if you had determination, heart, and community, you might just carve out something meaningful from the rough edges.

It showed me how to find joy in the small things. How to be resilient when everything around me felt unstable. That family isn't just blood, it's the people who feed you, check you, and show up when it counts.

Arcadia wasn't perfect. Neither was my childhood. But both were mine. Arcadia gave me the roots (and the toughness) I'd need when life later knocked me down in ways I never could've imagined. Before I ever stepped on a football field. Before I ever dreamed of life beyond my hometown. Before I found out what I was made of, Arcadia was shaping me. Teaching me how to take hits, get up, and keep going. I just didn't know yet how much I'd need those lessons.

Adversity has a way of stripping life down to the studs. It exposes what's real and what's fragile. It demolishes illusions but leaves behind something precious: the chance to rebuild, stronger and wiser than before.

The night I lay helpless on that field, I thought everything was ending. In some ways, it was. The version of my life I had clung to, the one where football was the centerpiece, was over.

But sometimes, losing the future you planned makes room for the life you were meant to live.

> Lesson 1: Home is more than four walls and a roof. It's family, friends, and community who love you, support you, and lift you regardless of circumstances.[IP]

2

WHEN FAITH FOUND ME

GROWING UP WHILE RAISING US

My mother, Andrea Lafon Shine, gave birth to me when she was just seventeen, still in the fragile space between adolescence and adulthood.

By then, she was already a mother to my older brother, Kiaeran, who was two years old at the time. Though we were born of different fathers, there was never a divide between us. From the moment I opened my eyes to the world, Kiaeran was my first friend, my constant companion, my mirror. We were tied at the hip, bound by blood and even tighter by love.

Kiaeran and Perris

Our mother was thrown into the deep waters of parenthood long before most of her peers had finished high school. She was still learning who she was, figuring out her identity, even as the world demanded that she be a provider, protector, nurturer, and disciplinarian all at once. It was a near-impossible balancing act, and yet she walked that tightrope with a quiet strength that I didn't fully appreciate until years later. She never complained. She never indulged in self-pity. Instead, she put her head down and went to work, literally and figuratively.

She held multiple jobs at once, hustling from one shift to the next, the soles of her feet aching and her eyes often heavy with exhaustion. She wore sacrifice like armor. Time and again, she chose to go without rest, warmth, and nourishment so that my brother and I could have what we needed. She bore the weight of our world on her shoulders and never once let it crush her spirit.

Perris and his mother, Andrea

Her days bled together in a constant hustle. It was an exhausting cycle of survival where sleep was a luxury and rest a forgotten dream. She was always chasing the next dollar, the next shift, the next breath of stability. In that relentless grind, childcare became more of a community improvisation than a structured plan. We were handed off like fragile parcels. Whoever had time, whoever had heart, whoever was simply available. Each day brought a new pair of arms, some gentler than others, some barely aware of the weight they were carrying. But through all that movement, all that uncertainty, there was one place that never changed. One place where love wasn't borrowed or conditional.

LOVE AND THE LORD

Our sanctuary was always our grandparents' home. That house didn't need a sign to tell you what it was. It *felt* like safety the moment you crossed the threshold. And at the heart of it all was my grandfather, Grandaddy P. He was the kind of man you write songs about. Stoic and smiling, his calloused hands always in motion and his heart always wide open. He worked when the sun told him to start and stop. Whether it was loading UPS trucks before dawn, hauling buckets in the nearby orange groves, fixing roofs under blistering heat, laying tile with precision, cutting grass in perfect lines, or rebuilding someone's patio just because they needed help, he did it all, and he did it with grace. Not once did he complain. Not once did his love waver. To us, he wasn't just a man; he was our first superhero. Bigger than life. Steadier than time. Grandaddy P was *everything*.

Perris in his grandfather's arms

And beside him stood my grandmother, the gentle anchor to his strength. She was a school nurse by trade, but truly, she was a healer in every sense of the word. Her touch, her tone, her very presence could mend more than scrapes and fevers. She soothed souls. She was the type of woman who had love stocked in every room, who made you feel like you were the most important person in the world just by the way she listened. Her care was never forced or performative. It was who she was, down to her bones.

Even with their own lives full to the brim, they never hesitated to step in. When life felt like too much, when the world outside felt too sharp or too cold, their home wrapped around us like a warm blanket. There, we could breathe without fear, play without watching our backs, and sleep without tension in our shoulders. It wasn't perfect, but it was home. And more than that, it was proof that even in the chaos, even when we were being passed between hands, love could be a constant. They made sure of it.

Despite always feeling loved, I was a scared kid. Not just jumpy, but deeply frightened. The kind of scared that settled into your bones and made your skin crawl at night. And it didn't help that my mom and brother had a taste for horror. I was too young to even understand half of what I saw, but they watched those movies like they were comedies. *Freddy vs. Jason. Wrong Turn. Jeepers Creepers. Gremlins. Anaconda.* Names that still echo in the back of my mind.

I'd sit there frozen, peeking through my fingers, pretending I was brave enough to watch, but inside, I was unraveling. I didn't just see the monsters on the screen. I *felt* them. I absorbed them. They followed me home in my imagination, slipped into my dreams, and made my nights stretch long and suffocatingly.

The dark wasn't just the absence of light. It was a presence. A heavy, lurking presence that filled every corner of my room. It crept beneath the bed, slithered behind the closet door, and hovered in the shadows. At night, my imagination turned my room into a battlefield. I'd lie rigid under the covers, heart pounding like a drum in my ears, eyes darting across the ceiling, sure that if I moved (if even a toe touched the floor), something would grab me and drag me away.

That fear changed the way I looked at the world. I didn't feel safe, not in the dark. Life felt unpredictable, like at any moment the world could twist into something dangerous. But somehow, in those long nights of terror, something else began to form inside me. Something small. Quiet. But solid. It was faith, and it started with my grandmother.

My grandmother was the calm in the storm. A woman who carried peace in her very presence. When the fear got too big, when I couldn't breathe, couldn't move, when my mind spiraled into the same haunted corners, she would come. No matter the hour. Her footsteps in the hallway were soft, but to me, they sounded like armor approaching. She would sit at the edge of my bed, gently take my hand, and say, "Let's pray." And together, we would whisper the Lord's Prayer into the dark like it was a weapon. *Our Father, who art in heaven...*

She promised me that whenever I was scared, if I closed my eyes and recited that prayer, God would protect me. That nothing could touch me while His name was on my lips. And I believed her. Not just because I wanted to, but because when she said it, I *felt* it. I felt something shift in the air. I felt covered. Seen. Safe. Her prayers didn't banish the fear completely. The nightmares still came. The shadows still moved. But now I had something to fight back with. Something stronger than the monsters.

Her faith wasn't performative. It wasn't a Sunday-only kind of thing. She lived like God was in the room with her, like she could see Him walking beside her. Church wasn't an obligation; it was her rhythm. Sunday services. Midweek Bible studies. Prayer groups. Her Bible looked like it had lived through a war, the way it was highlighted, underlined, notes in the margins, pages worn thin. She was a woman anchored in something far deeper than this world.

Looking back, I now realize the love my grandparents gave me, their patience, their grace, the way they showed up time and time again, wasn't just love. It was *spiritual.* It came from a well that didn't run dry. It was rooted in their unshakeable faith in Jesus Christ. It wasn't just kindness. It was a *covenant.* A sacred kind of love that carried me when I couldn't carry myself.

And my grandmother? She never let me forget where it came from. Not with words alone, but with how she lived, how she prayed, how she loved. She made God feel real. And in a world that often felt terrifying and unstable, *that* became my anchor. My safe place. My light in the dark.

A GLIMPSE OF THE DIVINE

Every Sunday morning, the world began before dawn. Before the sun spilled its first light across the neighborhood, my brother and I were already being nudged, shaken, and dressed as the clock's steady hands inched toward eight a.m. There were no exceptions, no excuses. My grandmother's quiet authority filled the house like a steady drumbeat: church was sacred, non-negotiable.

At five or six years old, church was something else entirely. It started as a heavy ritual I didn't understand, a slow march of boredom and restlessness. I would sit in those pews topped with blue cushions, the stiff fabric of my Sunday best scratching my skin, trying not to fall asleep. My head bobbed forward and back, a silent battle against the weight of drowsiness. The preacher's voice was a low hum, blending with the faint scent of polished wood and the distant rustle of hymn books.

But my eyes never stayed on him for long. Instead, I fixated on the clock above the door. Its face pale and round, the second hand ticking steadily away. I wasn't counting seconds for salvation. I was counting down to something far more tangible: the feast that awaited us after service.

Yams dripping in molten brown sugar, their sweetness a warm invitation. Collard greens, tender and smoky, seasoning that wrapped itself around your tongue like a hug. Ribs so soft they fell away from the bone with a gentle touch, and cornbread golden and crumbly, fresh from the oven's heart. And if luck smiled just right, a slice of sweet potato pie, still warm, its spicy aroma curling through the air like a whispered promise. That meal was my beacon. Church was just the toll to get there.

My perception of church began and ended with the aforementioned ideology until one Sunday, everything changed. It happened in the middle of worship, like any other Sunday, or so I thought. I had slipped into my usual routine, eyes half-closed, thoughts adrift in a fog of daydreams. But something caught me off guard. High above the stained-glass windows, where the rafters sliced shadows into beams, a light flickered. At first, I thought it was just the sun playing tricks, a prism bending through the colored glass.

But then the light shifted, grew, and from it emerged a figure sitting atop the massive white speakers hanging from the ceiling—radiant, delicate, and alive. Wings spread wide, shimmering with a glow that didn't belong to this world. I blinked, unsure if my eyes were deceiving me.

"Grandma," I whispered, nudging her hand. "Do you see that?" She glanced up, brow furrowed. "See what, baby?"

I looked back, the figure now hovering, so pure and gentle, like something out of a dream. She took my hand and squeezed it, her voice soft, as if telling me a secret: "Sometimes God reaches down in ways meant only for certain eyes to see."

In that breath, the air shifted. The church faded around me. The stained glass, the murmurs, and the worn hymnals blurred together, and all I could feel was that presence. A sacred hush, a personal touch from the divine, a call not shouted from the heavens but whispered into my soul.

SOMETIMES GOD REACHES DOWN IN WAYS MEANT ONLY FOR CERTAIN EYES TO SEE.

That moment etched itself deep inside me. I was no longer just a boy trapped in a pew, waiting for Sunday dinner. I was awake. Called by something greater, something real.

From that day on, faith was no longer a story I'd inherited. It was mine. The foundation I would build my life on. Nights still brought fear, and the dark still breathed threats, but now, I had words to fight back with. Whispered prayers slipped from trembling lips, a fragile lifeline when the shadows loomed too close.

Occasionally my mind painted other worlds. Brave worlds where I wasn't the scared kid hiding under covers, but someone strong and untouchable by fear. A place where the lights never flickered, where safety wasn't a wish but a given. Those worlds felt more real than the one I lived in, but even then, faith wove its thread through every breath. It grew beneath me like roots in the soil, steadying me when the ground shifted beneath my feet.

I didn't fully understand it then. But when I prayed, I felt steadied. When I remembered the angel, I knew that maybe I wasn't alone after all.

Lesson 2: Love is spiritual. It is a covenant based in faith in Jesus Christ. And this kind of love carries you when you can't carry yourself.[IP]

Lesson 3: Faith grows when you continually cultivate it through prayer.[IP]

3

SECRET SCARS AND PUBLIC FIRE

THE TRAUMA I TUNED OUT

Kiaeran and I were raised in a world that never promised steadiness. Our childhood was stitched together with uncertainty, with the ache of absence and the grind of survival. But woven just as tightly into that fabric was something sacred: resilience, passed down through blood and burden. From a mother who refused to break, no matter how hard the world tried. From grandparents who stood like anchors, unshaken in every storm. It wasn't an easy beginning, no. But it was *ours*. And from it, I learned how to recognize sacrifice not in grand gestures, but in the quiet surrender of comfort. I learned the quiet, unspoken strength of perseverance, and the burning, unwavering power of a mother's love.

It was one of those evenings that felt ordinary at first. One of those dusky, golden hours that slid into night with no warning, no fanfare. The kind of day you only realize is significant long after it's passed, when it no longer feels like memory but rather a scar that pulses under the skin.

My mother was working late, again. She always was. Stretching her hours like threadbare cloth, hoping to sew together a life that could just barely hold the three of us. Our grandparents, normally our soft place to land, had their own duties to tend to. And so, she turned to someone she trusted. A close friend. A queer man who had always been kind, always present, always dependable.

We were children then, Kiaeran was eight, and I was six. We were small, innocent, easily distracted by the flicker of a screen and the promise of joy. He had set up a gaming system for us, and my brother and I settled into it like it was our own tiny world. We sat cross-legged on the living room floor, controllers in hand, our laughter mixing with the electronic music spilling from the TV. The hum of the console was a comforting buzz beneath the soundtrack of childhood.

But as the night crept on, something shifted. Slowly. Subtly. The atmosphere thickened. The brightness of the room began to dim. Not because the light changed, but because the *energy* did. The way silence sometimes changes when a storm is building just outside the window. You can't see it, but your body knows.

He came to me softly, his voice gentle, too gentle. He said I looked tired and made it known that he knew I missed my mom. As a result of this, he offered the presence of his bed. It couldn't replace my mother, but it could suffice until she returned. I was six years old. Still soft around the edges. Still believing the best in everyone. And I *did* miss her. Always. So when he patted the bed and pulled the covers back, I went.

At first, it felt harmless. He pulled the blanket over us and spoke low, like a lullaby meant to soothe. But then his arm came around me, too slowly, too deliberately. His hand rested on my shoulder, then shifted. Lower. Wandering. It was small at first, like a question he was trying to ask without words. Then the movements changed. They became more certain. More wrong. His fingers searched places they were never meant to go, moving over my small body like insects crawling through tall grass. Each touch was a violation. Each breath from him was louder, more erratic, like a storm gathering speed inside a room that felt suddenly too still.

I didn't understand it. Not fully. But my body did.

My chest tightened like it had been wrapped in wire. My throat shrank. My breaths came thin and slow, as if even air had become dangerous. My eyes locked onto the ceiling, counting imperfections in the plaster, trying not to feel what I was feeling. The room smelled like fabric softener and something else. Something sour, something I still can't name but haven't forgotten.

I didn't cry. I didn't move. I simply *waited.* Waited for it to be over. For the nightmare to release me. I told myself I would be okay, even though everything in me whispered otherwise.

In the next room, Kiaeran slept in peace, safe in a sanctuary I couldn't reach. And between us, in the silence that followed, a canyon opened. One I never dared to cross.

I never told him. I never told anyone. Especially not my mother. She was already carrying the weight of the world in her arms. She was a young woman fighting every day to keep us afloat in a sea that never stopped rising. I couldn't hand her this. Couldn't place this ugliness at her feet and watch it poison what little light she had left. I feared it would break her. Or worse, that she would blame herself. And I loved her too much for that.

So I held it. Buried it deep. And I kept living.

I laughed when I was supposed to. Ate dinner at the table like nothing had changed. Played with my brother. Hugged my grandmother. I stayed a child on the outside, even while something inside me had already started to grow old too soon. But even in the silence, even in the hiding, something sacred flickered. Faith.

It didn't come with trumpets or thunder. It came in whispers. In late-night prayers spoken just above a breath. In the memory of an angel seen once from a pew bathed in stained glass light. It was quiet, yes, but it was *there.* Rooting itself in the dark. Becoming the foundation under trembling feet. And life, as it does, had other plans. But so did I. I would hold onto that flicker. And someday, I would turn it into fire.

THE DAY I BECAME A FIGHTER

That same year, another moment seared itself into me. One I wouldn't carry like a memory, but like a scar. I've always been a mama's boy. I wore my love for her like a second skin. It was undeniable, close, inseparable. To me, she was more than a parent. She was gravity. The warmth of the sun. The comfort of the moonlight. She was the center of my small universe, and being near her made the world feel right, no matter how chaotic it got. When she had a rare day off and brought my brother and me along for errands, I was over the moon just to be close. One stop, just one, she said. A quick visit to her boyfriend's apartment.

"Five minutes," she promised with a gentle hand on my shoulder, her voice soft, reassuring. "Just stay in the car." I nodded, even smiled. But as the door shut behind her, something inside me immediately tightened. The windows fogged slightly with our breath, the car quiet except for the hum of passing traffic. I watched the dashboard clock like it was my lifeline.

Five minutes passed. Then ten. Then fifteen.

With each second, the air in the car thickened. I couldn't name it then, but I *felt* it, this creeping, pulsing dread, like the shadows were whispering that something was wrong. My stomach churned. My palms began to sweat. It was more than worry; it was a knowing. A deep, primal instinct that pulled at me like a hook.

I looked at my brother, still distracted, then slowly opened the door. My little feet hit the pavement. I walked toward the apartment, heart slamming against my ribs, every sense on fire. As I turned the knob and stepped inside, the air changed. It was thick. Charged. Like the aftermath of a lightning strike.

And then I saw her. My mother. Being *beaten.*

I saw her being punched, kicked, and her body thrown around. In that moment, I was overcome with an anger I had no idea was possible, and fury filled my eyes. I froze, just for a second, everything inside me just... stopped. My initial freeze began to thaw as something boiled inside of me. Rage. A fury I didn't know I had, that I didn't even know was possible at six years old. It consumed me whole. My vision blurred, but my focus was razor-sharp. I didn't think. I moved. I sprinted to the kitchen, where my small hands grabbed the first thing I could find. The cold steel of a knife. The weight of it felt unnatural in my palm, but I held it like a sword, like justice, like vengeance.

I charged. I didn't know what was going to happen, and I didn't care. All I knew was that no one would hurt *my* mother. Not while I was alive. Not while I could still stand. But even as she was being brutalized, her eyes found mine. And in the middle of the chaos, in a voice I'll never forget, she screamed, "GET OUT! GO TO THE CAR!"

Her yell cut through everything, the noise, the rage, the world. Her command hit me harder than any blow ever could. I dropped the knife. My knees buckled. My feet moved without thought. I turned and ran out the door, back to the car with my heart slamming, lungs burning, tears carving silent tracks down my cheeks.

I climbed into the back seat and curled into myself, trembling. That day, something in me broke, giving birth to something that would alter the course of my life. In the quiet of that car, I made a vow. One that didn't need words to be real.

I promised myself that this would not be our life. I didn't know how. I didn't know when. But I knew with a certainty beyond my years that I would find a way. I would protect her. I would build something different. Something safe. Something *better.* But for a long time after, I didn't know what to do with that promise.

The rage never left. It simmered just beneath the surface, boiling over in classrooms, in playgrounds, in the quiet moments where I felt too small to change anything. I grew defiant. Combative. Unreachable. School became meaningless. I lashed out not because I didn't care, but because I *cared too much* and had nowhere to put the fire. I was just a kid who wanted life to be different, but had no idea how to make it so. And just when it all felt too far gone, God stepped in.

PLAYING WITH FIRE

When I was eight, I found myself alone in our small apartment while my mother tended to errands. I stumbled across a lighter and, out of curiosity, set a toy on fire. Fear took over. I panicked and threw the toy into the toy box, thinking somehow the flames would go out. Instead, they exploded. The box ignited. The fire spread. The apartment was consumed. By the time the flames were doused, the only thing saved from that fire was me.

At that moment, it didn't feel like God was guiding me anywhere. It didn't feel like a lesson in growth or destiny. It felt like failure. Like fear. Like I had single-handedly destroyed the one good thing we had. Mostly, I felt I had let my mom down.

Looking back now, with the benefit of years and perspective, I can see how even that disaster was a thread in a much bigger story. A story God was weaving, even when I couldn't see it. He wasn't setting fires to destroy me. He was allowing adversity to reshape me, to prepare me, to plant seeds of resilience that would one day bloom into something stronger than fear.

But as a kid standing in the middle of that smoke-filled apartment, I didn't see redemption. I saw only shame. I saw only my mother's face when she came rushing home, a mixture of panic, relief, and heartbreak. I saw how tired she looked. How much weight she carried. How much she had sacrificed just to give us a little better life, and how easily I had almost undone it all.

The blaze did more than destroy our home; it lit a legal firestorm. Child Protective Services became involved. My mother was charged with endangering me for leaving me alone. The court delivered an ultimatum: either my father, now somewhere in the picture, would take action, or I'd be placed into the foster care system. My mother fought tooth and nail in court, desperately trying to keep me. She fought my father. She fought the state. But while the adults battled over my fate, my life continued to unravel quietly in the background.

CHOOSING YOUR RESPONSE

Life will always throw things at you that you didn't choose. Hardships. Setbacks. Unfair circumstances. But while you can't always control what happens to you, you can always control how you respond. Choosing your response is one of the most powerful decisions you'll ever make. When life gets hard (and it will), you have a choice: Will you let the situation define you? Or will you define how you move through it?

It's easy to react out of anger, fear, or frustration in tough moments. It's easy to blame other people or even blame God. But real strength comes from taking a breath, stepping back, and choosing your response with intention. Will you be bitter, or better? Will you quit, or refuse defeat? Will you let the struggle bury you, or build you?

Your response can either lock you in a cycle of defeat or launch you into growth. It's not about pretending that everything's fine. It's about deciding that even when it's not fine, you won't lose who you are.

Every tough situation is an invitation, not just to survive, but to lead yourself with courage, character, and hope. Every moment you choose your response, you're building a stronger version of yourself. Life doesn't always give you a choice about the fight. But every time that bell rings, signifying another trial, another tribulation, every time your name is called, answer the bell. You don't have to win every fight; in fact, you won't win every fight, but you have to fight. That's how you win.

VISION BEYOND THE PAIN

In the midst of difficulty, it's easy to become consumed by the moment. Pain commands your attention. Disappointment distorts your perspective. Fear closes in, shrinking your view until all you can see is what's breaking right in front of you.

But true growth (true hope) requires something deeper. It requires vision. Not just for what is, but for what *could be.*

You have to look beyond the pain of today and dare to imagine the possibility of tomorrow. You have to believe, deeply and stubbornly, that your current reality does not get the final say. Because vision is what keeps your feet moving when everything else tells you to stand still. It's the quiet voice that whispers, *"This isn't the end,"* when every part of you wants to give up. It reminds you that the struggle is a page, not the entire story.

Without vision, you're held hostage by the *now*. But with it, you begin to see the *now* differently. Every delay becomes preparation. Every disappointment becomes redirection. Every detour becomes a lesson that strengthens the foundation for what's to come.

Vision isn't about denial. It's not unquestioning optimism or spiritual escapism. It's the ability to see *through* the moment, not just *in* it. To hold onto the belief that what is shaping you now is meant to carry you somewhere greater.

You don't get to choose how hard the journey becomes. But you *do* get to choose what you focus on. You can fix your eyes on the cracks in the road, or on the horizon that's still waiting for you. Vision isn't a luxury. It's survival. It's how you endure. It's how you overcome. And it's a constant reminder that where you are isn't where the story ends.

DURABILITY ON E, FUELED BY A PROMISE

The day of the fire didn't just mark destruction. It ignited something in me. That vow I made to myself that this would not be my life, not be my mother's life, became my fuel. One day, I would take care of her. One day, she wouldn't have to break her body just to keep food on the table. One day, she would finally know rest.

That promise lit a steady, persistent fire. Not like the reckless flames that tore through our apartment, but a different kind. One that warmed rather than burned. One that gave light when everything around me felt dark. That fire pushed me forward. It drove me to work harder, dream bigger, and believe that there was more to life than just surviving. I believed that, one day, we could actually live.

As I got older, my understanding of my mother began to change. I started to see her not just as a young, struggling mom, but as a force. A woman forged in adversity. A warrior in plain clothes.

She had once played football with the boys, and didn't just hold her own, she *dominated*. She was tough. Unapologetically competitive. Fiercely unyielding. Life tried to knock her down more times than I can count, but she kept getting back up, every single time. Her resilience was unspoken, but it was everywhere. In her eyes, in her hands, in the way she loved even when she was exhausted.

She taught me something essential: When life backs you into a corner, even when it feels like all the doors are closed, you still have a choice. You can either let the fire consume you or let it refine you.

I didn't always understand her decisions back then. As a child, I only saw her absence, her exhaustion. I saw the long hours and late nights. But with time came clarity, and with it, reverence. Because now I understand: It takes a different kind of strength to keep showing up when your gas tank is on E. To keep believing in better when the world gives you worse. And that's what she did, for my brother and me.

Her strength lit something inside of me. I've taken it with me through everything: injuries that nearly broke me, setbacks that threatened to define me, and disappointments that tested every ounce of my faith.

And that boyhood promise never left. It became the ember I returned to, again and again, fueled by a mother's example. Trials I never would've chosen refined it. And always, the quiet, steady hand of a God who was present, even in the fire, guided me.

MORE THAN A ROOF: WHAT FAMILY TEACHES US

No family is perfect. Every household carries its own history, cracks in the walls, unspoken wounds, quiet acts of love, and loud moments of pain. Some homes are filled with laughter and stability; others wrestle daily with chaos, dysfunction, or heartbreak. But no matter what shape it takes, family leaves fingerprints on the soul, marking who we become and how we navigate the world.

At its core, life isn't about square footage or bank statements. It's about people. About who shows up. About who stays when things fall apart.

You can live in a mansion filled with luxury, or a one-bedroom apartment where the lights flicker and the floor creaks, but if love doesn't live there, the space will still feel empty. You can have all the material success in the world, but if you have no one to share it with, what do you have? You're still poor in all the ways that count.

Community and authentic connection are not luxuries. They are necessities. We were created to need one another. Family, friends, neighbors, and mentors are the ones who help you remember who you are when the world makes you forget. They are the steady hands that lift you when life knocks the wind out of your chest. They help carry your burdens, celebrate your joys, and sit quietly beside you in your sorrow.

Somewhere along the way, many of us buy into the myth that strength means self-sufficiency and needing help is weakness. We're supposed to be invincible, unshakable, and impenetrable. But we were never designed to be Superman. We were made for connection. Needing help doesn't make you broken; it makes you human.

Even the strongest among us don't stand alone. They have people holding them up. Behind every resilient soul is a quiet army. People who prayed for them, guided them, encouraged them, and carried them. Trying to face life alone might seem noble, but in the end, it leads to exhaustion, isolation, and it slowly unravels the spirit.

It takes real courage to admit you can't do it all on your own. It takes strength to let others into your struggle. It takes wisdom to know that healing, growth, and joy are richest when shared.

Growing up, I didn't have much in the way of money. What I did have was wealth, although it was the kind that can't be counted. Cookouts that smelled like hope. Pickup games that taught teamwork. Front porch conversations that healed more than any therapist could. Those moments shaped me far more than any earthly possession ever could.

Because people matter more than things. More than zip codes. More than titles or trophies.

When you are rooted in a strong community, you're never truly without. Even when the bills pile up or the walls close in, you're rich, *in presence, in connection, and in legacy.* And legacy is what endures.

From the moment I took my first breath, family and community began shaping me. They laid the foundation for how I saw the world, how I loved, and how I responded to adversity. Not all of it was ideal. Some of it was deeply imperfect. But every moment, whether joyful or jagged, was part of the mold that shaped my heart and mind.

Even the broken pieces taught me something. From those pieces, I learned how to speak, love, navigate conflict, and stand my ground. A supportive environment instills confidence, while a chaotic one may teach resilience. Affirmation teaches identity. Struggle teaches strength. Some of us learn how to trust. Others learn to survive. Both are lessons.

But here's what I know for sure: Your beginnings don't determine your becoming.[IP] Your early environment may shape the story, but you still hold the pen. My flawed yet beautiful family taught me values that became my compass: integrity, grit, kindness, and perseverance. And yes, sometimes I learned those lessons through hardship, not comfort. But that's the paradox of growth: sometimes, what breaks you open also builds you up.

Even in dysfunction, character is forged. Even in absence, strength takes root. Even in struggle, legacy can be born.

The truth is, most families are a mix of pain and promise. But neither defines you entirely. What matters most is what you do with it, what you carry forward, what you choose to release, and how you decide to live differently.

Family may shape the beginning of your story, but the rest of the pages are left blank because only you can write them.

> Lesson 4: Affirmation teaches identity but struggles teach strength.[IP]

> Lesson 5: God allows adversity to shape your character and qualifies you for the future he has prepared for you.[IP]

4

DREAMS, DETOURS, AND DESTINY

FUEL FOR THE DREAM

The thought of creating a better life for my family and myself was the fuel that stoked my inner fire. I wanted to succeed so badly, not only because of the opportunities it would afford me, but, more importantly, because of the impact it could have on my mom.

For young Black men in my community, success didn't seem to have a thousand different doorways. It had two: football or basketball. Sport was the ticket out. It was the path everyone could see, the dream that felt just close enough to reach if you were fast enough, strong enough, lucky enough. If you wanted more than what our neighborhoods had to offer, you had to run for it, jump for it, or fight for it, whether on the field or on the court.

I ran to my grandfather one afternoon, bursting with the kind of wide-eyed certainty only a kid can have, and said, "I'm going to the NFL." He smiled at me, not the kind of smile that humors a child's fantasy, but the kind of smile that said, *If you're willing to work, I'll work with you.* He nodded and said simply, "Okay. Let's work on it." And so we did.

Every chance we got, we trained. In the backyard, at the park, on school ball fields that were more dirt than grass. We chased that dream together, throwing, running, sweating under the Florida sun.

To me, the NFL wasn't just a fantasy. It was hope. It was my way to prove that I could make something more of my life, and maybe take care of the people who had given everything for me.

SIRENS AND SEPARATION

One sweltering afternoon in Arcadia, the kind where the heat hangs heavy like a wet towel on your shoulders, my grandfather, my older brother Kiaeran, and I were at football practice with our little league team, the Dolphins. We were on the cracked, sun-bleached baseball diamond that sat right beside the old high school football field, nestled at the corner of SW Palm Drive and SW Hillsborough Avenue. The air shimmered with heat, the kind that made the grass crunch under your cleats and turned every breath into something thick and metallic. But none of that mattered.

Kiaeran and I were buzzing with energy, our excitement cutting through the humidity like a fresh breeze. This was no ordinary practice. It was the lead-up to our matchup against the Eagles, the undisputed powerhouse of the Desoto County Youth Athletic Association. They were the team everyone wanted to beat, and we were locked in, our minds sharp, our bodies primed. The field felt like a battlefield, and we were ready for war.

Without warning, the sharp wail of sirens sliced through the afternoon air. The entire field fell still. Red and blue lights danced violently against the sunlit haze as a fleet of police cars barreled toward us. Tires screeched. Dust kicked up in thick clouds.

The chaos was immediate and disorienting. Whistles stopped blowing, footballs dropped mid-spiral, and helmets hung limp in trembling hands. Every eye turned toward the flashing lights, scanning for answers, scanning for danger.

I remember how we all glanced at one another, quick, uncertain, and wide-eyed, as if searching each other's faces for some unspoken understanding of what was about to happen. In that moment, the game, the heat, the Eagles, everything disappeared. All that remained was the weight of the unknown.

In my community, the sound of sirens didn't mean help was on the way. It meant trouble was near. And more often than not, it meant someone who looked like us was about to be caught in it. Even as kids, whenever a police cruiser rolled by, a rhetorical question etched itself across all our faces, as visible as the sweat glistening on our brows: *What did I do wrong?* That day was no different.

The officers parked along the edge of the field and began fanning out, walking slowly from group to group, questioning the kids who'd only moments ago been laughing, running, and living in the freedom of youth. My heart pounded like a drumline in my chest. I kept thinking: *They've got the wrong place. They're looking for someone else. They'll figure it out before they get to us.* But they didn't.

The police cars kept inching closer until they finally stopped right beside the field I was on. One officer stepped out, approached my coach, and asked him to identify me. I saw the hesitation in my coach's eyes, the silent protest behind his furrowed brow, but eventually, reluctantly, his finger rose and pointed straight at me. My name was called. I froze.

My grandfather, standing on the sideline, immediately began walking toward us. Obvious confusion was written all over his face, but it was laced with something deeper. Fear. The officer looked me square in the eye, his voice flat and final: "You're going with your stepmother." My world cracked in half.

I didn't understand. I cried out, reaching for the only constant I had, my grandfather. I wrapped my arms around him like he was a life raft in a storm, sobbing into his shirt, refusing to let go. My voice shook as I pleaded, screamed, and kicked. I begged them to let me stay. None of it mattered.

What I didn't know then was that the state had been watching us. The fire in our apartment, the "unstable home," the nights we spent alone (things that had become normal for me) had triggered alarms in the eyes of strangers with power. They decided my mother was unfit to raise me. They decided my life needed to be ripped from the roots.

The officer picked me up like I was luggage, like I wasn't a little boy with a beating heart and a home I loved. He placed me in the back seat of a black Tahoe, the leather cold against my legs. As the doors shut with a thud, I twisted around and pressed my palms against the window.

Outside, my grandfather stood frozen. His shoulders slumped, and tears glistened in his eyes as he watched me be taken. The field, the kids, the noise, all of it crushed under the weight of what was happening. Grandfather didn't move. He couldn't. And as the car began to drive away, I watched him shrink in the distance, swallowed by the world that had just torn me from his arms.

One moment, I was wrapped in the warmth of my mother's love, my brother's jokes, and the safe, sturdy hands of my grandparents, the foundation of who I was. And the next, I was gone. Ripped away. No warning. No time to hold on. Just silence, and the cold, cruel absence of everything I called home.

A STRANGER'S HOUSE, A SOLDIER'S RULES

I found myself living with a man who, until then, had existed only in fragments. He was just a name on a birth certificate, a few worn photographs tucked away in drawers, and whispers exchanged in tense tones when grown-ups thought I wasn't listening. That man was now my father.

Beside him stood my stepmother, a kind woman, who stepped in and tried to be everything she could to me, even though I was not hers. Her daughter (my new stepsister) shared my space but not my heart. We passed each other like strangers in a bus terminal, connected by circumstance and little else.

To say I disliked them would be too kind. The truth is, I hated them, at least at first. My young heart couldn't see it any other way. They'd stolen me from the life I knew, from the tenderness of my mother's love and the comforting chaos of my brother's laughter, and cast me into a foreign land where I spoke none of the language. I was now a stranger in my own story.

My father, tall, stern, immovable, was the embodiment of military discipline. He was a man carved from order and rigidity, and he ruled our home with the precision of a drill sergeant. Structure wasn't a suggestion. It was gospel. Discipline, obedience, and work ethic were the air we breathed. It felt as though he wasn't just raising a son, he was forging a soldier. And me? I was nine years old.

Before the sun had even broken the horizon, he'd pull me from sleep and out into the biting dawn air. The grass, still damp with dew, soaked through my sneakers as I trudged toward the backyard. There, without explanation, I'd be ordered to move a heavy stack of firewood from one side of the yard to the other. Hours later, with my small body aching and blisters forming on my hands, he'd nod once, coldly, and tell me to move the logs right back to where they started. It wasn't about firewood. It was about control. About dominance. About breaking the wildness in me before it grew too loud. Like a wild horse being broken into submission, it was a test to see when I would break.

When I disobeyed or simply failed to meet his impossible standard, the punishments came swiftly. Grueling physical labor. Verbal lashings. When those didn't work, a leather belt became best friends with my hind parts. Hours spent reliving the mistake through sweat and tears chipped away at me slowly, like water wearing down stone. My muscles ached, and my spirit sagged under the weight of expectation. The space between us grew wider by the day, a canyon carved by silence, resentment, and pain. And yet, beneath all of the fatigue, the bruises, the sting of words I wasn't old enough to process, there lived a quiet ache, a longing I couldn't shake. It lived deep in the hollow of my chest and burned behind my eyes at night when the house went still.

THE SHERIFF'S STATION SILENCE

I missed my mother with a hunger that gnawed at my soul. It was an ache that no amount of sleep, food, or forced routine could dull. I missed her scent, soft and familiar like warm linen in the sun. I missed the gentle music in her voice when she called my name, the way her arms wrapped around me and made the world feel safe, even when it wasn't. Her love had been my anchor, and without it, I felt unmoored. Like I was drifting through days that felt colder and harder than they ever had before.

At night, when the house fell quiet and the weight of the day pressed down on my chest, I cried into my pillow, my whispers barely louder than the hum of the ceiling fan. I spoke to God in trembling tones, pleading for just one moment with her. Just a glimpse, a hug, a chance to feel whole again.

Eventually, a visitation schedule was arranged. A fragile thread of hope in a world that had gone dim. I'd be allowed to see my mother every other weekend. The plan was simple: my stepmother would drop me off at the sheriff's station downtown, and my mother would pick me up there. To me, it felt like a miracle. A window cracked open in a suffocating room.

The night before that first visit is branded into my memory. I couldn't sleep. My little bookbag sat zipped at the foot of my bed, packed days in advance with clothes, a toothbrush, and too many expectations. I lay awake staring at the ceiling, my heart racing with anticipation, picturing her smile, her laugh, the way my brother and I would pick up right where we left off. I could almost taste the meals she'd cook. The fried chicken, the mac and cheese, the love folded into every bite.

When morning came, we drove in silence to the station, my legs bouncing, my eyes glued to the road. Each car that pulled in made my heart jump. *Is that her?* I imagined her face behind every windshield, imagined the way she'd leap out of the car and run to me, arms wide open. But each time, it wasn't her.

Ten minutes passed. Then twenty. Then thirty.

Still no sign of her. We tried calling. We sent texts. No answer. An hour crawled by, and my hope thinned into something brittle. I sat in that metal chair at the edge of the waiting room, staring out across the parking lot, watching the horizon like it might give me an answer. But the truth settled in slowly, like dusk swallowing the light: she wasn't coming.

We drove home in silence. I pressed my face against the window, hot tears tracing lines down my cheeks. I didn't want my stepmother to see me cry. I didn't want to give her the satisfaction. I whispered to myself, *There must've been a reason. Something came up. She'll come next time.* But she didn't.

Visit after visit, I sat in that same chair, hands folded neatly in my lap, hope clinging to me like a wet coat. And every time a car pulled in that wasn't hers, my chest caved a little more. Each no-show etched deeper cracks into the foundation of what I believed about love, about trust, about what people meant when they said they'd be there.

Two years passed like this. Two years of waiting. Two years of tears pressed against car windows. Two years of unanswered questions that echoed louder with every visit: *Why didn't she come? Why wasn't I worth it?*

And then, just as I began to harden, just as I started to bury the pieces of myself that still hoped, everything changed again. I was ten years old. And the ground shifted beneath me once more.

UPROOTED AGAIN

I'll never forget the day my father told me we were leaving Arcadia, Florida. He said it casually, almost like an afterthought: "We're driving to Olympia, Washington." Just like that.

As if it weren't 3,219 miles away. As if it weren't an entire world apart from everything I had ever known. Just him and me, in a car, chasing orders he'd been given. Orders that would uproot the last fragile threads connecting me to my mother, my brother, and the grandparents who had helped shape the very core of who I was.

He was being stationed at Fort Lewis. And with that one sentence, the last hope I had of seeing my mother with any kind of regularity vanished like mist in the morning sun. She was gone. My brother, gone. My grandparents, those quiet giants of love and wisdom, were reduced to occasional voices on a phone and flickering memories I clung to in the quiet.

That move was more than just a relocation. It was a fracture. A shift. The beginning of a chapter I hadn't asked for. One that was colder, quieter, and lonelier than anything I'd ever known. A chapter written in long silences, unfamiliar streets, and the weight of becoming someone I didn't fully recognize yet.

But even as the distance stretched wider and the absence settled deeper, one thing remained constant: *the fire.* The fire to build something better. The fire to rise not just for myself, but for them. For the mother who had once been and still was my entire world. For my brother, who still laughed like the world was simple. For my grandparents, who had poured so much of themselves into me. The idea of giving them something more, *a new life, a new reality*, was the fuel that kept me going when everything else felt like it was falling apart.

I wasn't just trying to survive. I was trying to *rewrite history.* To be the break in the cycle. To become the bridge between who we had been and who we could still become.

Every step I took, every hard decision I made, was powered by that vision. It echoed in my head during early mornings, in cold air, beneath gray skies. It steadied me when my body ached, and my heart felt too heavy to carry. It reminded me, again and again: *You can't stop. Not now. Not yet.* Because this wasn't just about me. It was about *all of us.*

A PACT ON THE OPEN ROAD

The beginning of that cross-country journey was quiet, almost eerily so. Just the steady hum of tires against the asphalt, the occasional rustle of a snack wrapper, and long stretches of silence broken only by the low rhythm of the radio or the sigh of the wind. Outside the window, the flat, sun-drenched landscapes of the South slowly gave way to hills, then mountains, then the endless sprawl of the unfamiliar. I remember watching it all blur past, the world changing mile by mile, as if we were driving straight out of one life and into another.

At first, we didn't speak much. It was just me and my father, a man I was still trying to figure out, sharing the same air but not yet the same rhythm. But somewhere deep in the middle of the country, maybe it was Texas, or Kansas, or some nameless stretch of open road, something shifted. That's when he introduced what could be called "man talks." He turned down the music, looked over at me, and asked a question that settled deep into my chest like a stone dropped in water:

"What do you want to be when you grow up?" It caught me off guard. Not because I didn't know the answer, but because no one had ever asked me like it mattered. Coming from where I did, from the projects, the hood, the places people forget to name on maps, dreams like that didn't stretch too far. There were only a few ways out, and sports (especially football) felt like the most tangible one. It was more than just a game to me. It was a lifeline.

So I told him the truth. "I want to go to the NFL." He didn't laugh. Didn't smirk. Didn't wave it off like something childish I'd outgrow. Instead, he nodded slowly, his eyes fixed ahead, jaw set like stone. "Do you understand what that takes?" he asked. "I do," I said, meaning it. He looked over again, this time with something burning behind his gaze. "Then we start now."

And right there, in that car, somewhere on a road that stretched like a ribbon through the middle of America, we made a pact. A sacred agreement between father and son: to chase the dream, relentlessly, with everything we had, every single day. But he didn't let it stop there. He pushed me deeper.

He asked what I wanted to *do* with that dream. What I wanted it to mean. After a pause, the answer came, not just from my mind, but from somewhere deeper. From my spirit, maybe. "I want to go to the NFL," I said, "and use the platform it gives me to spread the word of God." That became the foundation of everything.

It was no longer just about success. It was about purpose. It was about turning pain into power, struggle into strength, and dreams into ministry. That car ride became my first altar. That conversation, my first calling.

Along the way, we stopped to see things I'd only ever read about in worn textbooks or seen in grainy school videos. We saw Mount Rushmore, Civil War memorials, dusty museums that smelled like old paper and time itself. They had always felt like fiction, like backdrops in someone else's story. But seeing them with my own eyes, standing there, breathing the same air as history, it shifted something inside me. If these places were real, maybe my dreams could be, too.

That road trip, just me, my father, and the vast, open road, expanded the boundaries of my world. It stretched my imagination. It made the future feel like something I could reach out and touch.

And then we arrived. Olympia, Washington. The moment we pulled into that quiet, manicured neighborhood, I felt it: *shock*. A cold slap of displacement. I had been yanked from a world of overgrown yards, sagging fences, chickens running loose, cracked pavement, and the thumping pulse of a community that felt like home, no matter how rough it was. Now I was surrounded by silence. Order. Perfect lawns trimmed like golf courses. Driveways lined with shiny SUVs. Streets wide enough to feel empty, and houses that all looked the same. It felt like a movie set. Or a dream I didn't belong in.

The faces were mostly white. The air felt different. Thinner, maybe. And no one looked like me. There was no transition. No easing in. No warning. Just a full-blown culture shock, sudden and staggering. I had entered a new world, one that didn't speak my language or know where I came from. I was the outsider now, carrying a dream, a purpose, and a past I couldn't let go of. But I had made a promise. And I intended to keep it.

FIELDS OF BELONGING

Football saved me. It was the start of the school year, and I was a stranger in a strange land. I was thousands of miles from everything familiar, everything warm. The air in Olympia was different. The kids talked differently. The neighborhoods looked like pages torn from a catalog I'd never been allowed to flip through. I felt like an outsider. Unseen, unspoken to, barely understood. But then came football.

Joining the Olympia Bears was my first doorway into something that felt like acceptance. Our first practice wasn't at some pristine stadium. It was at a dusty baseball diamond in a public park, the kind where grass grew uneven, and chalk lines faded beneath cleats. I stood alone at the edge of the field, my helmet dangling in my hand, scanning a sea of unfamiliar faces. Most of them were white. I was one of only a few Black kids out there, and I could feel the weight of that difference in every glance, every second of silence before the drills began. So I kept quiet. I stayed to myself, unsure of who I could trust, unsure if I even belonged. But then the whistle blew.

And when the ball snapped, and the play began, something inside me clicked. My feet moved like they'd remembered something my heart had forgotten: how to run, how to push, how to fight. My talent didn't ask for permission. It didn't wait to be welcomed. It *announced* me.

Speed. Power. Precision. My presence on the field spoke louder than words ever could. And people noticed.

What began as cautious glances turned into nods. Then smiles. Then dap after practice. Respect was earned, and with it came something even deeper—connection. For the first time since Florida, since being torn from the arms of my family, I felt something solid forming beneath me. Belonging. That acceptance didn't stop at the sideline.

It followed me into the hallways of McKenny Elementary School, where I started fourth grade with my head low and heart guarded. But my teammates began introducing me to their friends.

Lunchtime wasn't so lonely. Recess became familiar. And slowly, brick by brick, I began building a community. Not just as the new kid, not just as the Black kid, but as *me*.

I walked into that classroom with cautious optimism, still carrying the weight of the miles I'd traveled, the pain I didn't yet have words for. But I also carried something else: *hope*. Because for the first time in what felt like forever, I saw a path forward.

RACISM IN THE READING CIRCLE

It didn't take long before I came face-to-face with something I had never experienced so openly, so unfiltered, and so cruelly: *racism*. It happened during our school's "Reading Buddies" program. This was a well-meaning initiative where older students were paired with younger ones to help them read and connect. I was excited, eager even. My name was called, and

I stepped forward, ready to meet the first-grader I'd be paired with. He was a small white boy, no older than six or seven.

But as I approached, something in his face changed. He didn't smile. He didn't speak softly or awkwardly like most kids that age. He looked straight at me, lifted his hand as if stopping traffic, and said with chilling clarity: *"I'm not comfortable working with him... because he's Black."*

The words didn't just hang in the air. They *sliced* through it. The room fell deathly silent. Even the walls felt like they were holding their breath.

My stomach dropped. I stood there frozen, unable to move, unable to speak, as every pair of eyes turned toward me. I wasn't just a kid in that moment. I wasn't a fourth grader, or a football player, or a classmate. I was *Black*, and suddenly that was all anyone could see.

The teacher's face flushed with shock. She quickly sent the boy to the principal's office and said his parents would be called. She tried to smooth the moment over with hushed reassurances and a smile that didn't quite reach her eyes. But the damage was already done.

I felt exposed, like someone had stripped away every layer of who I was and left me standing there, raw and humiliated. I didn't fully understand the complexity of it, but I understood enough to feel it in my bones. That kind of rejection, so blunt, so public, so tied to something I couldn't change, cut deeper than I was ready for. It left a mark.

When I told my father and stepmother, their outrage was immediate. Their faces hardened. Their voices grew sharp. That night, the decision was made: I was transferring schools.

They enrolled me at Hansen Elementary, a school across town, known for being more culturally diverse. It was Olympia's cross-town rival, and to me, it felt like a lifeline.

Fifth grade at Hansen was a turning point. For the first time, I wasn't the only Black kid in the room. I wasn't *othered* by my appearance or the way I spoke. There were kids from all walks of life, and for the first time in Washington, I felt seen. Understood. *Normal.* And in that space of acceptance, something powerful began to grow inside me.

Football, which had always been my outlet, started to become something more: *my calling.* My training got serious. No longer was it just backyard drills or weekend games. I began to live it. I studied film. I ran hills until my legs burned. I did push-ups until my arms trembled. I began crafting the future I had promised myself and my father on that long drive west: the road to the NFL.

But now, I wasn't just running toward a dream. I was running *through* something. Through the pain of rejection. Through the sting of racism. Through the doubt that had once tried to define me.

And every sprint, every rep, every drop of sweat whispered the same thing in my ear: *You belong. You matter. Keep going.*

BUILT BY THE WORK

My father was a soldier through and through. Not just in uniform, but in the way he moved, the way he spoke, the way he demanded the world around him to operate. Discipline wasn't an option; it was oxygen. Structure, respect, and accountability weren't suggested; they were expected. Non-negotiable. Immutable. And if I didn't use my *mind*, he made sure I used my *body*.

Punishments in our home didn't look like timeouts or having privileges taken away. There were no gentle talks about consequences. No sitting in a corner to "think about what I'd done." No. My consequences came in reps. In burning thighs. In aching arms. In sweat-drenched shirts and trembling muscles.

I'll never forget one Sunday night in particular. I had brought home a bad grade. A C or a D, I can't remember now, but it didn't matter. In my father's eyes, anything less than excellence was failure. He called me into the living room, the soft flicker of a football game dancing on the TV behind him. The sound was low, but the tension in the room was loud.

"Sit on the wall," he said, meaning the dreaded wall sit. I took my position. Knees bent at a 90-degree angle, back flat against the sheetrock, legs already buzzing with anticipation. Then came the words I had learned to fear: "If you fall before I say, you're getting a beating."

Simple. Final.

Minutes passed. Maybe two, maybe five, maybe more. But for a kid, time stretches when pain is the clock. My legs shook, my eyes blurred, and eventually, I couldn't hold it anymore. I collapsed to the floor, gasping, defeated.

He stood up silently, walked across the room, and placed something in my hands: a leather belt I had come to know far too well. Its weight was small, but what it carried wasn't. Without yelling, without theatrics, he delivered the punishment, each strike carving a memory into my skin and spirit. When it was over, there was no debrief. No lecture. Just a command: "Back to the wall."

And I went. Back into position. Same rule. Same consequence. My body already raw, my legs barely steady, my pride somewhere in pieces on the floor. But I did it. Because that was the standard. That was the expectation. And in my father's world, expectations were not adjusted for emotion. They were met, or you paid for falling short.

It was brutal. It was relentless. But it carved something into me. A toughness. A refusal to fold. It taught me how to suffer with purpose. How to push when everything in me screamed to quit. And in a strange, complicated way, it *worked.*

Because when I ran hills in the rain, when I did pushups, pull-ups, and dips until my arms went numb, when I stared down adversity later in life, I already knew what it was like to break and keep going. I had learned it on the wall.

MORNING MILES, MIDNIGHT PRAYERS

As I got older, my life became a shrine to routine. Every day etched with the sweat of sacrifice, every hour accounted for like precious currency. My mornings began before the sun even considered rising. At 4:30 a.m., while the world still slept in silence, I would lace up my shoes, step into the chill of the dark, and run.

That first mile wasn't just a warm-up. It was a declaration. Each stride whispered, *You don't want it as bad as I do.* Then came the hills. Twenty sprints, each one a war between body and will. My legs burned, my lungs screamed, and with every step, I confronted the voice that begged me to quit. Pain became the teacher. Willpower, the lesson. Mechanics, the music.

When the sprints were done, I'd hit the field. Cutting, turning, exploding into routes with the precision of someone chasing more than just a game. On strength days, I traded the field for "20 Sets," a brutal gauntlet of pull-ups, dips, and pushups done to failure, and then repeated twenty times over. No mirrors. No crowd. Just me, gravity, and the voice in my head reminding me why I started.

Every drop of sweat was a prayer. Every torn muscle fiber was a brick in the foundation of a future I could barely imagine, but refused to stop building. Weakness had no seat at my table.

Then, I'd shower. Eat. Dress. And head to school. Exhausted? Always. But strangely, never more awake.

Academics began to carry a new weight. They weren't chores anymore; they were strategy. A good GPA was a highlight tape for the mind. It was a bridge to scholarships, exposure, and escape. I locked in. Dialed up. I even ran for school president and won. For the first time in what felt like forever, I felt like I belonged. Not just as a student, not just as an athlete, but as a young man on a mission.

But when the final bell rang, my day wasn't over. Far from it. I went straight to practice. Football, track, whatever sport was in season. Drills, sprints, technique, more sprints. Parachutes flapping behind me like the weight of my dreams, trying to slow me down. As the sun dipped behind the hills and teammates peeled off one by one, I was still out there. Cutting, grinding, chasing something unseen.

And when practice ended? I wasn't driven home. I was dropped off a mile away.

That last stretch? I ran it. Every time. No shortcuts. No complaints. Dead tired, yes. But too determined to let fatigue write the ending of my day.

Then home: dinner. Homework. A quick shower. And finally (finally), bed.

But sleep was never the best part of the night. What I looked forward to most happened in the quiet, when the house was still, and the world went dark. Those were my late-night conversations with God.

I'd lie in bed, eyes wide in the dark, and wait, maybe twenty minutes or so, until the silence felt deep enough to speak into. Then I'd talk to Him. Really talk. About everything. The girls I liked. The way they laughed. My dreams. My frustrations. How much I missed my mom. My brother. My grandparents. The ache of their absence.

And He listened. Or maybe I just believed He did. But it felt real. Like He was right there with me, responding not in words, but in peace. In understanding. In strength.

God became more than an idea to me during those years. He became my best friend. My confidant. The only one who truly knew just how much I was carrying. And alongside Him, I was falling in love with the work.

Not just the outcome. Not just the dream. But the grind. The process. The repetition that most people ran from, I ran toward.

The goal never changed: become the #1 running back in the nation. Earn a Division I scholarship. Excel in the classroom as much as I did on the field. And never, *never,* go back to where I came from, except to reach back and pull someone else out.

Those middle school years weren't just about physical growth. They were about the transformation of spirit, of character, of faith. Pain forged me. Persistence defined me. And possibility lit the path ahead.

ADVERSITY DOESN'T GET THE FINAL SAY

One of life's cruel ironies is that the very things we resist (the struggles we try to escape, the burdens that feel unbearable) are often the same tools that shape us into who we're meant to become. The same hand that felt too heavy at the time became the pressure that refined me. My father's rigid parenting wasn't easy to accept, but the way I responded to it would come to define me. Not with bitterness or rebellion, but with resilience. I didn't always carry the best attitude, but deep down, I knew: these trials were stretching me, not destroying me. In some crazy way, they were preparing me.

Adversity has a voice, and it doesn't whisper. It lies. It says you're not good enough, smart enough, strong enough. It tries to shrink your dreams down to something manageable, something safe. It convinces you that your goals are too big, your past too broken, and your efforts too small to matter. But that's exactly why belief is so crucial, why hope is so crucial.

Belief is your anchor when the world tilts. It grounds you when life feels unstable and unkind. It fuels your climb when the trail disappears beneath your feet. Belief makes you press on when logic tells you to turn back.

You must believe in the dream, even when it flickers like a distant star. Believe in your purpose, even when the world tries to bury it in doubt and detours. Most of all, believe in yourself. Not the person you pretend to be, but the one who's endured every storm and still refuses to lie down.

BELIEF IS YOUR ANCHOR WHEN THE WORLD TILTS.

Because that dream inside you wasn't planted by accident. It exists for a reason. You were built to rise, outlast, overcome, and endure. Not by skipping the struggle, but by surviving it. When adversity surrounds you, and progress feels invisible, trust the process anyway. Trust that the pain isn't pointless. Trust that the hardship is crafting a version of you strong enough to carry the blessing you haven't yet reached.

Growth doesn't come quickly, and strength isn't forged in peace. The slow, brutal, often lonely process is doing more in you than you can possibly see in real time. You must trust that the dark days aren't wasted days. Trust that the pressure is forming a version of you with shoulders broad enough to carry the future you were made for.

Adversity only wins when you stop believing. It wins when you give up just one step before the breakthrough. But when you keep showing up, grind through the silence, and work through the doubt, you rob adversity of its power. You take the pen back from the hands of hardship and let faith write the ending instead.

Trusting the process doesn't mean faking a smile or pretending you're okay. It means believing, even with tears in your eyes, that the struggle has a seat in the story God is telling through your life. It means choosing patience. Choosing faith. Choosing to keep fighting when every part of you aches for rest.

When you choose to trust, you protect your promise from being stolen by temporary pain. You keep moving. You keep becoming. And slowly, sometimes painfully, you step into the person you were always meant to be.

Adversity will tell you that hard work doesn't matter. That no matter what you do, it won't be enough. That success is for someone else. But that's a lie. Hard work *works.* Not because it gives you everything easily, but because it builds something deep inside you that adversity can't touch: character, discipline, endurance.

HOLD TIGHT TO YOUR VISION. WATER IT WITH PRAYER. GUARD IT WITH DISCIPLINE. FEED IT WITH FAITH.

Hard work is how you last. It's how you keep pushing when the odds are against you. It's how you keep breathing when life has you gasping. Every rep in the dark, every mile when no one is watching, every hour spent grinding when quitting would be easier, that's where the story is built. That's where you win.

Adversity may slow you, bruise you, or even bend you, but it only breaks you if you let it. It only wins if you stop believing. So hold tight to your vision. Water it with prayer. Guard it with discipline. Feed it with faith. Don't hand the pen to adversity. Don't let hardship dictate how your story ends. Because in the end, it won't be the ease of your path that defines you. It'll be your refusal to give up.

Looking back, one of the greatest ways my family shaped my future was by forging my emotional resilience. Life will test you, and I learned early how to survive the trials without succumbing to them. Family teaches a child how to feel deeply, how to fall and rise, how to turn pain into wisdom and heartbreak into fuel. My parents and my brother, through encouragement or confrontation, helped shape my identity. Their presence, and sometimes their absence, gave me the clarity to know what I wanted to become.

Even those raised in fractured homes can grow into greatness. Adversity, for all its pain, sharpens your edges and deepens your hunger. Some of the strongest people I've known came from the most broken beginnings. Success wasn't handed to them; they earned it despite everything stacked against them.

Because family doesn't define your limits, it introduces you to them. It's your response that determines whether those limits break you or build you. And if you're willing to confront them, forgive where needed, and rewrite the story, then you can become the cycle breaker. You can be the one who says, "It stops with me." Therapy, mentors, faith, and hard work all help in writing a new chapter. And I chose to do exactly that.

Every family has storms. Every family faces hardship. But purpose is the light that shines beyond survival. When your world feels heavy, you have to reach back. Back to the why, back to the calling, back to the dream that first made your heart beat faster.

Adversity wants you to forget that dream. But if you hold onto it, guard it with grit, protect it with prayer, then not even adversity can stop you. You were born for more. And the fire you walk through now? It's not the end. It's the forge.

PURPOSE IS GREATER THAN PAIN

Purpose gives your pain a pulse, breathing life into your suffering and reminding you that the ache has direction. That the battle has meaning and you're being reshaped by the storm.

Without purpose, pain feels like punishment. It spins you in circles and whispers that you're stuck; it says that life is random, unfair, and void of reason. But when you're anchored to a deeper *why*, everything changes. You recognize that the chaos carries a structure.

Purpose transforms adversity into a force that builds you. It shapes struggle and gives it teeth. Purpose gives you strength to walk in the dark.

When your lungs burn, and your muscles scream, and your soul feels like it's crumbling under pressure, purpose holds you together. Purpose whispers, "Keep going." Not because it's easy. But because it matters.

When the reps burned too long, or progress seemed invisible, I reminded myself of my purpose. When it appeared I was chasing a dream that ran a step ahead of me, I remembered that purpose mattered. I wanted breakthroughs. Instead, I got inches. I got slow, painful steps. And yet, I kept moving.

Purpose taught me something the world often forgets: Who you become on the journey is more important than reaching the destination. Sometimes success is as simple as refusing to stay down. You need to drag yourself out of bed when quitting would be so much easier. You must hold onto faith when everything around you screams that hope is naïve.

And those quiet, defiant, ordinary moments are the essential elements of every success story. Each one is a declaration: "I will not let adversity write the ending to my story."

Martin Luther King Jr. once said, "If you can't fly, then run, if you can't run, then walk, if you can't walk, then crawl, but whatever you do, keep moving forward." Because any movement is resistance, rebellion against despair. It is a refusal to die where you stand.

So don't despise the crawl or dismiss the steps that feel too small to matter. Those are the bricks that build a legacy. They form the foundation that proclaims your purpose to the world.

One day, you'll look back, realizing that what you thought were your weakest moments were the ones that made you unbreakable. Not because you sprinted the whole way. But because you *never stopped climbing*. And that? That is how purpose wins. That is how you win.

> Lesson 6: You may have a dream, but you must turn it into a purpose.[IP]

> Lesson 7: Believe in yourself. Believe in your purpose.[IP]

5

FROM UNDERDOG TO UNSHAKEN

MISS BATEMAN'S RULER AND A WORD THAT STUCK

At Memorial Elementary in Arcadia, my report cards were warning signs rather than a reflection of what I was capable of. It wasn't because I lacked intelligence. I knew that much. It was because I simply didn't want to be there. School felt more like a sentence than an opportunity. It was a place where I was told to sit still when everything inside me needed to move and stretch beyond the edges of the desk that confined me.

I wasn't a bad kid. I was just restless. And if I could trade boredom for a moment of laughter, whether at my own expense or the teacher's, I took that trade every time. The classroom was a stage, and I made myself the headliner. The problem was, I didn't realize the cost of my performance.

Then came third grade. And with it, a woman named Miss Connie Bateman. Miss Bateman wasn't just a teacher. She was a presence. She carried herself with authority but wasn't harsh. Stern, yes. But never cold. Her voice could quiet a room without raising in volume, and something in her gaze told you she wasn't to be tested. Not because she didn't care—but because she cared too much to let you waste yourself.

My mom and grandparents, in their deep-rooted faith in discipline, gave her permission to set me straight, however she saw fit. I laughed it off at the time. What could she possibly do? I found out.

One day, I was up to my usual antics, trying to turn the classroom into a comedy club. Miss Bateman warned me once, firm but fair: "Perris, you'd better stop before I get you." But the truth was, I didn't believe her. I was invincible, the show-runner of the classroom. I smirked and kept going. Then she called me up to the front.

I walked down that narrow aisle like it was a runway, chest puffed out and a defiant grin carved across my face. The class leaned in, waiting for the showdown. I didn't realize I was walking straight into a lesson I wouldn't forget.

Without hesitation, Miss Bateman pulled out a ruler and delivered a sharp, stinging swat across my backside. The pain wasn't the worst part. It was the laughter. But this time, my classmates weren't laughing with me. They were laughing at me. And for the first time in a long time, I didn't feel like the star of the show. I felt like a fool.

After class, with the sting still fresh and my pride in pieces, Miss Bateman called me aside. She looked me dead in the eye. But there was no anger there, just honesty. And something else. Something deeper. Belief.

"Perris," she said, "you're smart. You can be somebody. But you've got to act right. You've got to apply yourself. You have too much potential to waste."

She said it like she meant it, *knew* it. And in that moment, I saw myself, maybe for the first time, through someone else's eyes. Not as a class clown, but as a kid with something real inside him. Someone worth shaping. Someone worth saving.

That moment didn't flip a switch, but it did plant a seed. And seeds, given the right pressure and light, grow into trees that stand for decades.

Slowly, I started to shift. I started completing my homework. I stopped treating school like a joke and started treating it like a chance. A door. A way forward. Because maybe, just maybe, it wasn't a prison. Maybe it was a platform.

SEEDS, GIVEN THE RIGHT PRESSURE AND LIGHT, GROW INTO TREES THAT STAND FOR DECADES.

Miss Bateman was the first person in a school building who didn't just correct me. She *believed* in me. She saw beyond the behavior; she saw the potential. And she made sure I saw it too.

That spark she lit? It didn't just stay in the classroom. It grew into the fire that fueled my work ethic for years to come. A fire that burned through excuses and lit the path toward everything I would become. She taught me one of the most important lessons I've ever learned: Discipline without belief is punishment. But discipline rooted in love? That's transformation.

ORDERS FROM THE PENTAGON, PLANS IN THE DUST

By the time I reached high school, I was no longer the restless, unfocused kid I had once been. I had evolved. The mischief had hardened into drive. The need to be seen had transformed into a hunger to be *respected.* My work ethic had sharpened into a blade. Relentless, precise, and untouchable. I was locked in. And it showed.

Eighth grade had been a breakthrough year, and for the first time, everything felt like it was finally falling into place.

My little league team, the Capital Cougars, had just won the championship. I was surrounded by teammates who felt like brothers. School was smooth. My grades were solid. I had a routine, a rhythm, and a purpose. For once, life was clicking.

There's a specific kind of peace that comes from alignment. When your surroundings reflect your ambition, when your days begin to stack into momentum. That was where I was. Aligned. Focused. Ready. And then, boom. Another move.

My father had received new orders. This time, a reassignment to the Pentagon in Washington, DC. And in the snap of a finger, everything I had built was swept out from under me. No warning. No conversation. Just boxes, goodbyes, and the hollow ache of starting over again.

I didn't want to go. Not when the road ahead finally felt clear. Not when I had real plans.

I had dreamed of attending Capital High School, suiting up in black and gold, winning a state title with the same teammates I'd grown up with, and launching myself into a Division I career. I had mapped out the path like it was scripture. I could see it all so clearly. Every game, every accolade, every step. It wasn't just a fantasy. It felt inevitable.

But that vision? It shattered the moment we packed the last box into the moving truck. I watched the world I had built disappear in the rearview mirror, helpless to stop it. And that's the thing about being a kid in a military family. Your life is never really your own. You learn to adapt, adjust, and say goodbye so often that it starts to feel like a reflex. But just because you get used to it doesn't mean it stops hurting.

That move taught me a brutal lesson: Even the best-laid plans are fragile. Stability is not a promise; it's a privilege. And just when you think you've arrived, life can reroute you without asking for permission.

But here's what I've learned since: You can mourn the plan *and* still move forward. You can grieve what was lost while building something new. Because sometimes, the detour leads to the destination. And if your purpose is strong enough, no relocation, no redirection, no unexpected blow can rob you of where you're meant to go.

It took time, but I learned how to turn disappointment into fuel. To let go of what *should have been* and focus on what *could still be.* Because my dream didn't die with that move; it just changed zip codes.

A STAR IN A LOSING CULTURE

When we landed in Virginia, I enrolled at Osbourn Park High School in Manassas. On the surface, it looked like any other public school. Brick hallways, crowded lunchrooms, a marching band echoing faintly from the practice field. But beneath that ordinary exterior was a football program steeped in hopelessness. The team hadn't won a game in over ten years. Not one. The weight of that failure clung to everything. It stuck to the locker room, the practice field, the players' eyes. You could feel it in the air, heavy and stale. Defeat had become part of the school's culture. Still, I came in hungry. Focused. Locked in. I wasn't there to adopt anyone else's mindset. I was there to shift it.

It didn't take long for the coaches to notice. I was outworking everyone in summer camp. I was the first to show, last to leave, chasing every rep like it held the key to my future. The varsity coaches wanted to move me up right away. But my father, ever the tactician, shook his head. "Develop first," he said. "Master the level you're at before you jump to the next."

So I stayed on JV. And we didn't just win—we *dominated.* I was a man possessed, waking up at 4:30 a.m. to train, studying film like it was homework, grinding through every drill as if to keep others from taking my spot. On the field, I felt like myself again. I was thriving. Off the field, however, was a different story.

Osbourn Park wasn't only plagued by a losing record. It was poisoned by a racial climate that ran deep and unspoken. I was called the N-word more than once. Sometimes whispered, sometimes barked loud enough for others to hear. No one flinched. No one stepped in.

One day during Spirit Week, a white student showed up wrapped in a Confederate flag like it was part of his wardrobe. Another flew one from the back of his pickup, driving slow laps around the school parking lot like he was parading a trophy. There was no confusion in their message, no attempt to hide the venom in their symbolism. It was deliberate, proud. And it was tolerated.

There were the smaller wounds; violations dressed as pranks or jokes. I remember walking into PE and realizing my phone had been stolen from my locker. No investigation. No apology. Just another reminder that I wasn't safe. Other times, kids would take my things or mess with my gear, little acts of cruelty designed to make sure I never got too comfortable. And the worst part? The silence. Not from the students. I expected that. But from the adults—the ones who were supposed to protect the students. Their silence was deafening.

It didn't take long for my parents to see it for what it was. This place wasn't going to nurture or elevate me. It was going to break me down, piece by piece, until I either quit or became someone I wasn't. Osbourn Park wasn't a platform; it was a ceiling. And I was already scraping my head against it. Halfway through the year, I transferred to Bishop Ireton, a private

Catholic school in Alexandria. There, I donned a new uniform and started again.

Perris playing for the Bishop Ireton Cardinals

Bishop Ireton became a turning point—a test wrapped in a blessing. I was still undersized and underestimated, but I earned respect by carving out a name for myself with grit, toughness, and performance that no one could ignore. In the classroom, I excelled. In time, I saw my reflection change. Not just in the mirror, but in how the world responded to me. On paper, I was thriving. But something beneath the surface was shifting.

After experiencing the open hostility, the silence that followed it, and the constant need to prove I belonged, success started to feel heavier, as if it came with a cost. Every yard I gained on the field, every A I earned in class, was a brick I had to lay to build my own worthiness. I was fighting to exist fully, freely, and unapologetically. That kind of fight leaves a mark on your soul.

The lesson? Sometimes progress isn't only about moving forward. It's about surviving what was meant to stop you. And the scars? They prove you're still standing.

THE PORCH AND THE PAIN

I began to notice the growing gap between my world and everyone else's. While my peers were going to parties, holding hands in hallways, sharing secrets under glowing streetlights, I was stuck in a loop: school, training, more training, home. That was it. I was grinding as if my future depended on it, because in my mind, it did. But deep down, I couldn't ignore the ache that I was missing something essential. A piece of my youth was slipping through my fingers like water I couldn't cup tightly enough to hold.

So I started chasing it. Not recklessly, just desperately. I wanted a taste of the life everyone else seemed to be living so effortlessly. I longed for a moment at a school dance, or a shy smile exchanged with a girl in the hallway. A joke during lunch that made someone laugh. These tiny things most kids didn't think twice about felt like rebellion in my world. But my parents didn't see it that way. Instead of loosening the reins, they yanked them tighter.

The 4:30 a.m. alarms screamed at me daily. I ran before school, sat through classes, then went straight to football practice. From there, I hustled to AAU track workouts to refine my speed, sometimes not leaving the track until the sky had gone completely dark. Then it was home, homework, a few hours of sleep, and repeat.

People noticed. Teachers. Coaches. Even neighbors. They pulled my parents aside, gently suggesting they ease up and give me some breathing room. But their words fell like rain on stone. Nothing soaked in.

And if I stepped out of line, even slightly, the punishment was swift and severe. If my tone wasn't cheerful enough, if my body language hinted at exhaustion or frustration, I paid the price. Wall sits until my legs trembled. Push-ups until my arms gave out. Yard work under the blazing sun. Raking leaves until my palms blistered. Chopping wood until I could barely lift the axe. And then came the worst of it.

My father would drive me to the highway exit near our home, drop me off without a word, and make me run the ten miles back. After school, after two practices. It wasn't a workout. It was a test. If I didn't make it home before everyone else was asleep, I wasn't allowed inside. I slept on the porch. Cold. Filthy. Alone.

Even silence became dangerous. I wasn't disrespectful. I wasn't even loud. But in our home, quiet wasn't strength. It was seen as defiance, rebellion without words.

Once, I said I missed my mother. Just that. Just truth. And he beat me for it. My stepmother saw my longing as betrayal, as disrespect toward her effort to raise me. But the ache for my mom wasn't a rejection of her. It was the child in me still hoping for comfort, for something soft in a world that had become so hard.

Junior year, we made it to the state championship game against Benedictine. It would be a rematch, another chance to finish what we had started the year before. I was hungry and focused. I was ready.

And then I heard it. Barely audible beneath the roar of the stadium, like a memory carried on the wind. "Perris."

I froze. That voice, I knew it. It was her. My mother.

I hadn't seen her in years. Suddenly, the lights, the field, the game, everything vanished. All I could see was her. My body was on the field, but my spirit had already run toward her.

That night, I didn't play well. We lost. And honestly? I didn't care. Because for the first time in what felt like forever, my mother had come to find me.

After the game, I rushed out of the locker room. I scanned the crowd. I searched the shadows. But she was gone. I begged my father and stepmother to call her. Eventually, they did and put her on speaker. My father asked if she could come by, just so I could see her. She said no. He pleaded. Still, no.

I was shattered. A silence wrapped around my heart that words couldn't pierce. What had I done to deserve this distance? Why did love feel like a privilege I hadn't earned? In that moment, I was that same little boy all over again. Crying in a police department parking lot, waiting for a mom who never came. But I did what I always did: I swallowed the pain and kept moving. Until one day, I couldn't anymore.

SON TO SLAVE

My breaking point? Snapchat. That's all. I just wanted to download the app like everyone else. I wanted to talk to a girl. I didn't want to feel policed, or punished, or alien. So I made a fake email account and downloaded it. When my stepmother found out, the storm broke.

She told my father. That night, he came home, sent the rest of the family upstairs, and looked at me like I was a stranger. "Get completely naked," he said. Then: "Lie down over the couch." I obeyed. Numb. Terrified. "I'm going to beat you like a slave until I get tired." And then he did.

He lashed me with a leather belt until my skin split and welts raised across my back. I later sat in a bathtub filled with Epsom salt, staring at the white tile, trying not to scream as the sting burned into every open wound. I remember thinking: *How can someone do this to their own child?*

Something inside me cracked that night. Not like a branch in the wind, but more like a dam. Everything I had buried, the pain, the confusion, the fury, it rose to the surface and demanded to be heard. When the house fell quiet, I ran. Out the back door. Down the street. No destination, just away.

I made it a mile before my AAU track coach, who had become more of a father than the man who raised me, pulled over and picked me up. He gave me a bed. Food. Safety. Then he looked me in the eyes and said words I'll never forget: "A man faces what he fears. But I won't let them hurt you again." I didn't want to hear it. I hated how true it was. But he was right.

The next day, he took me back home. Of course, my parents wore their masks. Concerned. Soft-spoken. Measured. But as soon as my coach drove away, the act crumbled.

My stepmother snapped. She shoved me. Choked me. Threw books at me. Screamed that I was a disgrace. I didn't fight back. I didn't cry. I didn't run. I just stood there. Still. Silent.

Because by then, I had learned: in that house, I wasn't being raised. I was being broken. I wasn't a son. I was a prisoner. A servant. A slave.

A LIGHT IN THE LOCKER ROOM

During one of the darkest stretches of my life, when home felt more like a battleground than a place of refuge, the football field became my sanctuary. My coaches were the closest thing I had to help me find peace. Few truly grasped the weight I carried, but men like Coach Tony Verducci saw through my disguise. He was more than just a head coach at Bishop Ireton. He was a compass, a second father. He showed up for me not just in cleats and game film, but in spirit. He believed in the boy buried beneath the bruises and expectations, and in doing so, helped shape the man I was becoming.

Perris as a Bishop Ireton Cardinal

Coach Verducci never let me coast. He didn't coddle, but he cared. He demanded excellence because he knew I deserved to see what I was capable of, not because he was hard. In a world that often punished my voice, he gave me space to speak.

When the chaos of home threatened to swallow me whole, his belief became my lifeline.

But just before my senior season, that anchor was ripped away. Coach Verducci was fired, caught in the crosshairs of school politics that had nothing to do with football and everything to do with ego. It gutted me. Playing without him felt impossible. I considered walking away from the sport entirely. But even in his forced exit, he never stopped looking out for me.

Knowing what was at stake, he pointed me in the direction of Episcopal High School, a prestigious boarding school with both academic muscle and athletic tradition. It was a leap, a shot in the dark. But I took it. I applied and got in. And just like that, I stepped into the final, and most defining, chapter of my high school life.

BREATHING ROOM AND BREAKTHROUGHS

Episcopal wasn't just a school. It was air. For the first time, I could exhale. No more 4:30 a.m. alarms. No more silent punishments or walking on eggshells. I wasn't afraid to speak, laugh, or be curious. I could simply be. I was still accountable, still grinding, but now I had room to grow. For the first time, I could imagine a version of manhood that wasn't shaped by fear or force.

On the field, I became unstoppable. Episcopal gave me a platform, and I ran with it, literally and figuratively. I led my team to a championship and racked up accolades that once seemed unreachable:

- Three-time First Team All-State
- Two-time First Team All-IAC

- 2017 IAC Offensive Player of the Year
- Over 2,500 rushing yards in a single season
- DC Touchdown Club Player of the Week
- All-Metro Honorable Mention, three years running
- By graduation, I had rushed for over 5,000 yards

Perris at Episcopal High School

I was electric on the field. Tough, consistent, and deadly with the ball in my hands. My highlight reels stacked up against anyone in the country. I had the stats. I had the tape and the leadership. But there was one thing I didn't have—size.

At five foot six and 160 pounds, I didn't fit the prototype. Recruiters were chasing giants, not grinders. They overlooked me because I didn't look the part. In a sport that worships height and weight, heart too often gets left out of the equation.

No matter how many yards I ran for, how many defenders I shook, how many blocks I broke, I couldn't make myself taller. Couldn't weigh more without compromising speed. I was everything you wanted on paper, except for the paper itself. I wasn't a Ferrari. I wasn't built for the showroom. I was a Honda Civic, unbreakable but no flash. I was dependable and built for the long haul. But in a system obsessed with glitter, grit is often ignored.

And yet, it was grit that had gotten me to this point. Not talent alone. Not size. Grit. Grit earned me every yard, title, and ounce of respect. Grit kept me going when I was sleeping on porches, when my voice was silenced, when my back stung from belts, and I still got up and ran ten miles home. Episcopal didn't just launch my football career. It helped me reclaim my life. And while the world kept asking whether I was enough, I kept showing them I already was.

CLOSED DOORS AND OPEN WINDOWS

I believed I had an ally in Coach Panos Voulgaris at Episcopal, a man with a reputation for launching players to the highest echelons of college football. His name was synonymous with opportunity. Notre Dame, Michigan, Ohio State, Purdue, South Carolina, Georgia, these powerhouse programs were as familiar on our campus as the classrooms themselves. At a place like Episcopal, coaches didn't just lead teams; they fought relentlessly to open doors, championing their players with everything they had.

Later, I uncovered a truth that hit me like a sledgehammer to the chest: Coach Voulgaris, more concerned with protecting his own reputation than mine, had been quietly blocking my path. When top-tier programs showed interest, he downplayed my abilities, casting doubt on my potential, steering them away like a gatekeeper guarding a threshold I had every right to cross. He didn't believe I belonged at that level, and he made absolutely sure everyone else knew it too.

The betrayal cut deep. It was shocking, disorienting. A coach is supposed to be your fiercest advocate, your unwavering champion, not the biggest obstacle between you and your dreams. I could have crumbled beneath that weight. I could have let bitterness consume me. But I refused. That pain fueled my passion. I would not let anyone else dictate my limits. If anything, my resolve hardened. I doubled down on my dreams and my belief that my story was far from over.

Coach Voulgaris had his own plan: if I wanted to play, he told me, I should head to Yale. He made calls, reached out to their position coach, and arranged a visit. Yale wanted me. They saw what Coach Voulgaris didn't. They pursued me with genuine interest.

As I navigated the admissions process with laser focus, ready to forge my own path, fate threw me a curveball. The day before I was to sign my commitment letter, I got a call that stopped me cold, from Coach Howell at the University of Virginia.

It was unexpected, a long shot. I'd never taken an official visit to UVA. The only time I'd set foot on campus was for a fleeting 7-on-7 tournament. Hardly the exposure that leads to serious offers. Yet here he was, calling me at the eleventh hour.

"I can't offer you a scholarship," Coach Howell said plainly, "but I can give you a shot. Walk on. Whatever you earn, you keep."

It was a gamble. But gambling on myself had become second nature. I'd been doing it my whole life. So I said yes. I walked on at UVA fueled by a quiet, unbreakable belief that I mattered, that I could be more than a name on a roster, that I could fight for my place, and that I belonged on that field just as much as anyone with a scholarship.

That moment wasn't just a choice to play football. It was a declaration: I would write my own story. No gatekeeper, no doubt, no broken promise would define my journey. I was here to prove that heart, grit, and relentless belief can outshine any shadow cast by doubt.

LESSONS CARRIED FORWARD

Despite the tangled, often painful history between my father and me, he gave me two gifts I carried into that next chapter like armor: an unyielding work ethic and the relentless will to run until my legs screamed to stop, and then keep running anyway. Those gifts weren't just lessons; they became survival tools, the foundation of everything that followed.

Walking onto a Division I football program isn't for the faint-hearted. It's a lonely battlefield, a brutal test of grit where every day feels like climbing an endless mountain. You have to outwork, outlast, and out-believe everyone around you just to carve out a sliver of recognition. And I was ready to show them.

My high school stats, awards, and grades tell part of the story. The visible milestones. But behind every number, every accolade, stood a tribe. Coaches and mentors who saw past the surface, who believed in the restless kid who once couldn't sit still in third grade. They challenged me, held me accountable, and refused to let me settle for less than my potential. They taught me a truth I continue to carry deeply: belief alone is fragile. Without sweat, consistency, and relentless discipline, it crumbles.

Looking back, the thread weaving through my journey is clear as day. From Miss Bateman's sharp rap of a ruler on my backside to the floodlit intensity of Friday night games, two unwavering constants framed each stitch of my journey: belief and discipline. They walk with me still.

No victory is scripted in bold headlines alone. It's etched in the grind of pre-dawn mornings and the ache of late nights. In the quiet corrections of stern teachers and the steady guidance of patient coaches. In the second chances you don't expect but desperately need. For me, victory came to a kid who, despite every obstacle, chose to believe he could overcome his circumstances. That choice, simple, fierce, relentless, is the true beginning of every triumph.

> Lesson 8: Progress is about moving forward as well as overcoming the obstacles meant to stop you.[IP]

> Lesson 9: Progress is about continuous progress, always moving forward in the face of the adversity meant to stop you.[IP]

6

BUILT FOR THE CLIMB

WELCOME TO WILL DEVELOPMENT

Training camp. July. Freshman year. Pain.

That last word is the first word that surfaces when I think back to training camp. Not the kind of pain you nurse with an ice bath or sleep off with a few hours of rest. This was soul-deep, bone-aching, spirit-breaking pain. It was the kind of pain that makes you question why you ever signed up in the first place, and dares you to quit.

I'd always prided myself on being a hard worker. No workout ever felt too long. No rep too heavy. But this? This was unlike anything I'd ever faced. Our strength coach, Shawn Griswold, wasn't simply sculpting our bodies; he was forging our minds. He called it *Will Development*. It wasn't about how much you could lift or how fast you could run. It was about who you became when everything in you screamed *stop*, and the only thing keeping you moving was something deeper than muscle—your will.

From the first moment, everything had purpose, down to the uniform: white shirt, white shorts, white socks. We weren't individuals, just blank slates with our names scribbled across the chest in black Sharpie. We weren't people yet. We hadn't earned that status. Griswold lined us up in formation outside the locker room, ready to run. If one guy stepped an inch out of line, we were sent back. We tried again. Another misstep, again. Over and over. That's how we spent our first day: not practicing, not lifting, not playing, just trying to finish the *warm-up*. And even *that* felt impossible.

Every movement had to be synchronized. One person out of rhythm, and we started from zero. You weren't just responsible for yourself. You were responsible for the man beside you. That kind of pressure either breaks people or binds them.

There were no freebies. Everyone had to make their times. If one guy didn't, we *all* paid. If someone showed up late or loafed through a drill, the entire group bore the weight. Slowly, through sweat and failure, frustration and fire, a group of strangers began to morph into something tougher. A team, unified by suffering and shaped by standards.

Coach Mendenhall had a strike system. One mistake? You earned 365 burpee box jumps. That's not a typo. Three hundred sixty-five. At 5:00 a.m. With one hour to complete them. Miss the mark, and you came back the next day and tried again. Regardless of how wrecked you were afterward. The regular team lift still followed. The message was brutally clear: *one mistake = 365 chances to prove you won't make it again.*

Coach had his own brand of discipline. He believed that, just like applying for a job, you had to *interview* to earn your place on this team. But these weren't sit-down conversations. They were gauntlets. Gauntlets meant to show who you really were. We hurled sixty-pound medicine balls toward the uprights like our lives depended on it. We pushed three hundred-pound sleds, then six hundred-pound sleds, across one hundred yards of turf that felt like it stretched into forever.

I remember one session with Chayce Chalmers, Joe White, and me with a six-hundred-pound sled. Joe cramped up halfway through the rotation. Trainers rushed in with water and mustard. I turned to Coach, told him I'd push the sled alone and let the others rotate out. He didn't even hesitate. "No," he said. "No one's going to save you. Figure it out."

And so they did. Joe and Chayce pushed the final 40 yards, bodies breaking down but pride holding strong. That was the standard. No excuses. No shortcuts. No sympathy. Just relentless expectation.

Looking back, as brutal as it was, I understand that wasn't training; it was transformation. Coaches Mendenhall and Griswold weren't building football players. They were carving out character. Etching discipline into our bones. Instilling a level of grit and unity that most people will never taste. At UVA, you earned your jersey but also your identity.

THE LIFE OF A WALK-ON

The Bible says in Mark 9:35, "Anyone who wants to be first must be the very last, and the servant of all." I was about to learn the true meaning of that verse. Stepping onto a college football field as a walk-on is a feeling I still struggle to put into words. There's no spotlight. No roar of applause. No welcoming committee. Just a quiet tension in your chest and the sound of cleats against turf reminding you that you don't belong. Not yet. Maybe not ever.

But I wouldn't trade it for anything. That experience brought out parts of me I didn't know existed. It taught me to endure, to sharpen my edges, to stay rooted even when no one was watching. It built a resilience that was earned.

Most people don't understand the divide. There are two different realities in college football: the world of scholarship players and the world of walk-ons. Scholarship guys are the golden children. Handpicked from high school huddles and seven-on-sevens, groomed through stars and rankings. Coaches know their names before they step on campus. They're welcomed with open arms, thousand-dollar gear packages, tours, orientation dinners, and a sense of belonging baked into every interaction. And then, there's us.

The walk-ons. The ones without a scholarship, a stipend, or even a guarantee that we'll make it through camp. No cameras. No headlines. We show up fueled by nothing but belief and the need to prove that we belong. We pay for our education out of pocket. We earn no perks, no benefits, no special treatment. We fight for scraps of attention, hoping someone, anyone, sees the work we're putting in. We are, in every sense, *on our own.*

I came in ready for the grind. The early mornings, the conditioning, and the discipline were nothing new. My father had raised me for this kind of fight. I was built in adversity. Sharpened by pressure. But what I wasn't ready for was the silence. The invisibility.

Not being doubted, I could handle that. I *welcomed* it. But being ignored? Being treated like I didn't exist? That stung deeper than any hit I ever took.

There was no welcome dinner. No locker with my nameplate. No personalized gear bag waiting for me. No campus tour or photo ops. Just a quiet, unspoken message: *stay in your lane.* I remember walking into the facility for the first time and watching scholarship players laugh with coaches, dap up strength staff, and move like they belonged. I was a ghost moving through that building. No one told me where to go.

No one looked my way. There wasn't a map or manual for my path. I had to carve it out myself.

As walk-ons, we weren't seen as players in development. We were place-holders. Practice bodies. Human shields for the starting lineup. While the scholarship guys were being molded into stars, we were the tackling dummies that kept their uniforms clean. We weren't taught the full playbook. We weren't included in late-night film sessions or invited to the team events at Coach's house. We were outsiders, grinding in the shadows, hoping our moment would come, *if* it ever came at all.

But we knew this going in. That's what made us different. We weren't chasing handouts. We were clawing for respect.

And yet, nothing could fully prepare me for what it felt like to give everything, every ounce of strength, sweat, and will, and still go unnoticed. To execute your rep with perfection, only to watch the coach's eyes skip right over you. To feel like your effort was vapor, dissolving before anyone could see it.

We were invisible until something went wrong. And then suddenly, *all* eyes were on us. That's the life of a walk-on. You're not just fighting for a spot. You're fighting to exist.

PUBLIC SHAME, PRIVATE FIRE

There was one moment during my second year that shattered everything I thought I understood and rebuilt me in the process.

We were deep into practice, the usual rhythm unfolding like background noise. Walk-ons don't get called up. Not for real reps. Not when it matters. We're there to hit, not to play. To blend in, not to break through.

Then, out of nowhere, I heard it: my name. My number. Barked loud across the field by my position coach. Time slowed.

I hadn't been taught the play. I'd never seen that formation, never repped that set. Not because I hadn't studied or shown up, but because no one had ever expected me to be *there*. Walk-ons don't get put in those situations. We weren't groomed for that moment. We were invisible. But when life calls your name, ready or not, you *show up*.

I jogged onto the field with my heart hammering in my throat. Lined up. Wrong, just as I feared. Panic flickered in my chest. The ball was snapped, and for a beat, I froze. Feet stuck. Mind blank. I didn't know where to go.

The offensive coordinator lost it. A man I'd seen around but who, until that moment, hadn't even bothered to learn my name. "What are you doing?" "You don't belong here!" "You're wasting everyone's time!" "Get off my field!"

Each word hit like a stone to the chest. The field fell quiet except for his voice, echoing through my skull. My position coach, someone I had looked to for guidance, *laughed*. Not a word of encouragement. Not a hint of grace.

I stood there, exposed. Humiliated. Eyes on me. A nobody in a jersey, a body that didn't belong. My face burned. My chest tightened.

But somewhere beneath the shame, something else sparked. A low, steady flame that started to rise in defiance. That was the moment everything shifted. I remembered the words of Paul in 1 Corinthians 15:10: "But by the grace of God I am what I am, and his grace to me was not without effect. No, I worked harder than all of them—yet not I, but the grace of God that was with me."

I didn't crumble. I didn't quit. I *decided*. Right then and there: never again would I give someone else the power to disqualify me. If I were going to succeed, it wouldn't be because I was chosen. It would be because I refused to be overlooked.

Because I built my shot from the ground up, with my own two hands. That night, and every night after, I became *obsessed.*

I started sneaking into the facility under the cover of darkness, quiet enough not to trip the alarms, late enough to avoid the staff, early enough to slip in before the janitors arrived. I'd sift through trash cans for crumpled play sheets the scholarship guys tossed aside without a second thought. What they discarded, I devoured. I memorized formations, motions, audibles, checks, every scribbled note, every route tree, every backside read.

I watched teammates log into the film system and learned how to study like them. I snuck in film sessions solo, rewinding clips for hours, connecting what I saw with what I read. I ran hills at 2 a.m., my breath the only sound in the night, each step hammering in a new version of myself. I drilled footwork in parking lots lit by flickering floodlights. I recreated every blown rep in my mind, over and over, until my body *refused* to get it wrong.

I stopped trying to fit in. I started building myself into something they couldn't ignore. Stronger. Sharper. Faster. Smarter. I began dominating workouts. I won every rep. Every sprint. Every drill. I left teammates gasping and coaches with no excuse left to keep me invisible. And still, nothing.

No nod. No rep. No acknowledgment. But this time, it didn't break me. I didn't *need* recognition anymore. Because I knew what they hadn't realized yet: I was no longer asking for a shot. I was *taking it.*

Perris at UVA

A SCHOLARSHIP—BUT NOT A SHOT

For three years, I lived in the shadows. No spotlight. No fanfare. No roaring crowds waiting for my number to be called. Just the grind. Silent, relentless, and mostly thankless. A handful of scattered special teams reps were the only glimpses of the field I saw. But eventually, after years of fighting for every inch, I was awarded a scholarship.

Perris under the lights at UVA

It should've felt like validation. Proof that the sacrifices, the sleepless nights, the uphill battle hadn't been in vain. And for a moment, it did. But I didn't want congratulations. I didn't want claps in the team meeting or a post on social media. I wanted to *play*.

Going into my senior year, everything was lining up. I had the best spring of my career: crisp reps, explosive plays, consistent execution. I followed it with an even stronger training camp. For the first time, the buzz around me wasn't about work ethic. It was about performance. Coaches told me I was in the rotation and would get meaningful carries in the season opener. I was finally on the brink of *playing*.

So I waited. Helmet on. Chin strap buckled. Heart pounding in my chest like a war drum. I stood on the sideline, eyes locked on the field, waiting to hear my name.

It never came. Not in the first quarter. Not in the second. Not once all game. Not a single offensive snap.

And then it happened again. And again. Game after game, I stood there, ready, prepared, deserving, and was passed over. I felt myself fading into the background again, dissolving into that familiar place walk-ons go when the game forgets you. Except this time, I wasn't a walk-on anymore. This time, I *had* done everything right. I had earned it. I knew I belonged. And still, I was invisible.

That pain cut deeper than any hit I'd ever taken. It wasn't just rejection. It was erasure. And for the first time in a long time, I broke.

I called my mother. We had only recently reconnected after years of silence. My voice cracked as I told her I was done. That I had poured every part of myself into this game, and I had nothing to show for it but heartbreak and exhaustion. She listened. Quietly. Patiently.

Then she said something simple. Soft. Steady. "Hold on. God's going to send a sign." And a few days later, everything changed.

Our head coach, Bronco Mendenhall, stepped down unexpectedly. It was a shock. Coach Mendenhall had always struck me as unshakeable. The calmest man I've ever met. He didn't raise his voice to assert dominance. Only once, in all my years, did I hear him shout, and it was just to quiet the room. He led with a cool, composed authority. Stern, never harsh. Compassionate, but never indulgent.

He believed in standards. Clear, unwavering, and immovable. You either met them, or you didn't. No warnings. No demotions. If you fell short, you were gone. Not out of spite, but out of principle. His world was defined by structure and earned trust. I respected it. I still do. But part of me also wondered if that structure had left no space for someone like me.

So when he left, something inside me stirred. Maybe faith, maybe instinct, maybe both. *Maybe this was the door I'd been waiting for.* A clean slate. A fresh set of eyes. A new way forward. Then came Coach Tony Elliott.

From day one, he said the words I'd been waiting years to hear: "No favorites. The best player will play." Those six words were oxygen to a drowning soul.

Coach Elliott carried a different energy. Where Coach Mendenhall moved with surgical precision, Coach Elliott moved with visible passion. His emotions weren't masked. They were worn proudly on his sleeve. You could feel his investment, not just in your ability, but in your *story*. He coached the athlete but saw the human being.

He talked to us, not at us. He listened, checked in, and asked about more than just football. His youth showed in how he connected, but his standard remained crystal clear. He didn't tolerate mediocrity. Instead, he demanded greatness. He chose to lead with *heart* rather than with stoicism.

Mendenhall led like a tactician: methodical, unshakable, principle-first. Elliott led like a believer: emotional, engaged, people-first. Both men demanded excellence. One sharpened you with cold steel, while the other lit a fire in your chest.

TWO COACHES, ONE BIG LESSON

Coach Mendenhall and Coach Elliott couldn't have been more different. Funny enough, I needed *both* of them more than I ever realized. When I first started working under Coach Bronco Mendenhall, I thought I was ready. I believed I had what it took to compete at a high level. But in hindsight? I was still raw. Eager, yes. Hungry, absolutely. But unrefined. I hadn't yet been *sharpened.*

Coach Mendenhall didn't sugarcoat anything. He didn't throw out compliments or soften the blows. His standard was excellence. Unwavering, non-negotiable. He didn't care if you were a five-star recruit or a walk-on with no nameplate on your locker. If you didn't meet the expectation, you didn't play. Simple as that.

At the time, it was tough. I watched other guys take the reps I longed for. I battled feelings of jealousy, frustration, and confusion. I didn't understand why he pushed us walk-ons so relentlessly when, in the end, we weren't even guaranteed a place on the field. It felt like grinding in complete darkness, sweating, straining, sacrificing, all without a spotlight in sight. But that darkness? That silence? That's where the real transformation happened.

Coach Mendenhall taught me a lesson I carry with me to this day: fall in love with the work, not the reward. The value isn't always in the recognition. Sometimes, it's in the quiet moments. Those lonely lifts, early mornings, and late nights when no one is watching, and you still give everything you have. That's where character is built. That's where identity is formed. And then, just when I had finally learned to embrace the grind, *Coach Tony Elliott* arrived.

By the time Coach Elliott took over, I was a different player and a different person. My skills had evolved. My mentality had matured. I wasn't just hungry anymore. I was ready. And almost poetically, Coach Elliott created the kind of environment I had dreamed about during those hard years under Mendenhall. It was encouraging. Energizing. *Empowering.*

Coach Elliott brought heart. He led with emotion and connection, seeing the *person* behind the player. He coached with compassion but demanded excellence. His belief in us was vocal, visible, and *felt*. And for the first time, I didn't just feel prepared. I felt seen.

And I rose to the occasion. I earned a starting role. I scored touchdowns. I made the plays I'd visualized in my head for years. I became the player I always believed I could be.

Perris on the UVA gridiron

But here's the twist no one prepares you for: when I finally found myself thriving in the environment I used to *wish for*, I started to *miss* the one I once dreaded. That quiet, relentless pressure. That silent demand for more. The invisible hand that never coddled, only carved.

The intensity of Coach Mendenhall's approach, the structure, the discipline, the solitude of his standard, had shaped me in ways I didn't fully understand until I was standing in the spotlight, performing on the stage I used to beg for.

THE HARD SEASONS, THE ONES WHERE IT FEELS LIKE NO ONE SEES YOU, THOSE ARE THE ONES PREPARING YOU FOR THE MOMENT *EVERYONE* WILL.

In the end, each coach gave me exactly what I needed, *precisely when I needed it.* Coach Mendenhall taught me how to *work.* Coach Elliott gave me the *opportunity* to let that work speak.

I didn't fully appreciate it back then. But now? I see it with crystal clarity.

If I could speak to any young athlete fighting through doubt or obscurity, I'd say this: The hard seasons, the ones where it feels like no one sees you, those are the ones preparing you for the moment *everyone* will. Stay locked in. Trust the process. Embrace the grind. Because sometimes, the coach who's toughest on you is the one who believes in you the most.

FINALLY, MY NAME WAS CALLED

I threw myself into the grind all over again, body, mind, and soul. There was a new system to learn, and I attacked it like my life depended on it. Late nights in the film room, early mornings in the weight room, hours upon hours buried in playbooks and footwork drills. I trained like I was behind, like I had something to prove, because I did. And this time, something was different. For the first time in my career, I wasn't just being tolerated. I was *being seen*.

Coaches were noticing. Teammates were nodding. I felt momentum building, the quiet swell of something real. I had worked my way to the edge of opportunity again, and I was ready to leap.

Then, just three days before our first spring scrimmage, everything came crashing down. I tore my hamstring. Third-degree. Just like that, I was out. Spring camp? Gone. My moment? Gone. At best, I'd be cleared a few days before the spring game. The timing couldn't have been more cruel. It felt like the rug had been yanked from under me, again. But I'd been here before. Disappointment wasn't new to me. Pain didn't scare me anymore.

I lived in the training room. First one in, last one out. I attacked rehab with the same obsession I once poured into earning reps. Ice baths. Resistance work. Isometrics. Mobility drills. Whatever it took. I did it. And when I was finally cleared, days before the spring game, I wasn't anywhere near the top of the depth chart.

Didn't matter. I didn't need a title. I just needed *one* carry. And when that carry came? I made it count.

First touch of the spring game. I took the handoff, saw daylight, and exploded. Hamstring intact. Vision sharp. Legs churning like pistons. I cut through the second level, untouched, and 75 yards later, I was in the end zone. Touchdown.

The crowd erupted. My teammates went wild. And me? I smiled. Not out of surprise, but relief. After everything, I still had it.

Celebrating the big play

Fall camp arrived, and I didn't let off the gas. I had the best camp of my life. I was explosive, consistent, and undeniable. Every drill. Every scrimmage. Every rep. I made it all count. And finally, after years of being overlooked, passed by, or written off, I earned a starter position.

In my first career start, I rushed for over one hundred yards and scored two touchdowns. I became the first UVA running back in over a decade to do that in their debut. But it wasn't just a stat line. It was *vindication.*

Perris on the field

It was worth every sleepless night and hearing every no or whisper that I wasn't good enough. It was worth enduring every injury, every ounce of sweat poured in empty rooms, and every tear shed in silence. It was proof that I hadn't just waited for a shot; I *created* one. I kept walking when the path twisted or disappeared.

I fought for that moment. Bled for it. Prayed for it. And when my name was finally called, I *answered.* Not because the odds were in my favor. But because I had *never stopped believing* that one day, they would be.

THE UNWELCOME TEACHER

Adversity doesn't knock. It barges in. It shows up uninvited, often at the worst possible time, and forces us to confront parts of ourselves we might've otherwise ignored. Whether it's heartbreak, failure, loss, rejection, or some unseen battle deep inside, adversity is the great leveler. No one escapes it. But what separates those who merely survive from those who rise is this:

What do you do when life says no?

It's easy to see adversity as a detour, a cruel interruption to the path we planned. But in truth, adversity *is* the path. It's the pressure that reveals what's real. The discomfort that demands our growth. The test that sharpens our character and unmasks our values. We don't get stronger by cruising through life untouched. We get stronger by enduring the storm and learning to walk through it without losing ourselves.

When everything feels unfair, when your progress is invisible and your efforts unrecognized, it's tempting to look sideways. To compare your life to someone else's highlight reel. You see people who appear to glide past obstacles, gifted with advantages you never had. Maybe it's talent. Maybe it's money.

Maybe it's a support system you've only dreamed of. Whatever it is, it makes you wonder: *Why not me?*

But here's the truth: comparison is a thief. It will rob you of joy, peace, purpose, and identity. Every time you chase someone else's dream, you lose sight of your own. And here's what I learned the hard way: You can't win a race you were never meant to run.

I had to stop asking what everyone else had that I didn't, and start asking what I *did* have that I was ignoring: grit, hunger, vision, my voice. My internal compass that reminded me, over and over again: *Stay true. Be real. Run your race.*

And when I finally did, things began to shift. Not instantly or dramatically. But deeply. Because I stopped outsourcing my worth to other people's opinions and started trusting my own.

Let me say plainly: the loudest voice in the room doesn't deserve your allegiance. The truest voice in your head does. Some people will tell you you're not good enough. Others will tell you you're destined for greatness, but only if you do it *their* way. Both are distractions if they pull you away from your authentic path.

And then there are the gatekeepers. The coaches who overlook you, the bosses who undervalue you, the teachers who mistake potential for rebellion. They make the climb harder. That's real. But what they don't realize is this: Harder isn't the same as hopeless.

THE LOUDEST VOICE IN THE ROOM DOESN'T DESERVE YOUR ALLEGIANCE. THE TRUEST VOICE IN YOUR HEAD DOES.

Sometimes resistance is the what that builds your strength. The struggle doesn't reveal your limits; it expands them. You don't need to pretend adversity is fair because often it isn't. But you also don't need to give it the final word. That power belongs to you. Always has. Always will.

So what's the takeaway? When life gets hard, and it *will,* don't retreat. Don't compare. Don't crumble under the weight of someone else's expectations.

Rise anyway. Move forward with intention. Trust the process even when it hurts. Run *your* race. Not perfectly, but authentically. And let adversity become the fire that forges your future and your *foundation*. In the end, life doesn't test you to see if you can win; it tests you to see if you'll *show up*.

> Lesson 10: Fall in love with the work because the reward isn't always in the recognition. Sometimes the reward isn't in accomplishing the goal; sometimes it's who you become on the journey to pursuing it.[IP]

> Lesson 11: Comparing yourself to others robs you of joy, peace, purpose, and identity because when you chase someone else's dream, you lose sight of your own.[IP]

7

THE TRAGEDY

A GAME, A LOSS, AND A SHIFT IN ENERGY

It was one of those weekends you don't see coming. The kind that starts like any other, and ends by shifting everything. We were nearing the end of the season, worn but hungry, still chasing redemption. That Saturday, we went head-to-head with Pitt. It was supposed to be a battle. Instead, it turned into a nightmare.

From the opening whistle, chaos took the reins. On the first play from scrimmage, our quarterback, Brennan Armstrong, dropped back with confidence, eyes scanning the field. The ball left his hand, and just like that, disaster struck. Intercepted. Returned for a touchdown. A collective gasp rippled through the stadium.

Shaking it off, we lined up again. *One mistake. It happens.* But then, the unthinkable happened. Second snap. Same result. Another interception. Another pick-six.

Fourteen points. Sixteen seconds. We weren't just down, we were stunned. Silenced. Shellshocked.

The air in the stadium thickened with disbelief. It wasn't just the scoreboard that turned on us. It was the crowd. Boos poured down like a cold, sudden rain. You could feel the weight of frustration. Fans gripped their heads, coaches paced, and teammates looked around as if hoping someone, anyone, could hit rewind. And we still had 59 minutes of football left to play.

I won't walk you through every play that followed. There's no poetry in the kind of unraveling that took place that day. Drives stalled. Momentum died before it even had a chance to breathe. Each possession felt like climbing uphill in sand, and by the time the clock mercifully struck zero, we stood under a scoreboard that read 37–7.

It wasn't just the loss that stung; it was the *way* we lost. That kind of defeat gets under your skin. It lingers, gnawing at your pride. Still, sometimes the most humiliating days become the most clarifying.

That week, something shifted in us. No one had to say it because we all felt it. The embarrassment. The urgency to reclaim something we'd lost. So we got to work. The locker room wasn't filled with noise. It was filled with purpose. Every rep was sharper. Every drill carried weight. We weren't just practicing. We were preparing for redemption, for respect, and for each other.

Something about being knocked down that hard forces you to choose: stay down, or rise with intention. And we rose. Not because the world believed in us. But because, for the first time in a long time, we believed in each other.

A KNOCK IN THE NIGHT

November 13, 2022. It was a Sunday night draped in stillness with the quiet that settles in like a blanket after a long week; the air was cool, the world was slow, and everything felt suspended in peace. I had turned in early, lights off, body tired, mind softening into rest. It was the type of evening that lets you exhale, if only for a moment.

Bang! Bang! Bang! A thunderous pounding shattered the silence, jerking me from sleep. My heart jumped before my eyes even opened. It was the kind of knock that doesn't wait for an answer. It was urgent, relentless. I stumbled toward the door, still half-dreaming, and cracked it open.

Ronnie Walker stood there, wild-eyed and chest heaving. My teammate, my roommate. But in that moment, he looked like someone standing on the edge of something too big to name. "You seen Mike?" he asked, his voice taut with fear. Mike Hollins. Our third roommate. Another running back. My brother.

I rubbed the fog from my eyes, trying to pull myself fully into consciousness. The clock on the wall glowed with a late hour, one that ruled out any normal reason for this wake-up call. I tried to play it off, offering something casual. Maybe Mike was out blowing off steam. Sunday night fun. A girl, a bar, something harmless.

But Ronnie didn't even blink. No chuckle. No exhale. "Nah, bro," he said, shaking his head. "Something's *wrong.* No one's seen him. No one's seen any of them." A chill slid down my spine. Not fear. Not yet. Just unease. A gut feeling that something wasn't right.

I stepped out of my room and walked a few paces to Mike's. Knocked. Nothing. I opened the door slowly.

Dark. Still. His shoes weren't by the bed. No hoodie on the chair. No bag tossed in the corner. It looked untouched. Empty in a way that made my chest tighten. He was gone.

Ronnie and I moved quickly. We threw on sweats, grabbed keys, and headed into the cold night. The campus was silent, like a set after everyone's left. We checked everywhere: bars, lots, dorms, backroads, any place we thought he might be. Our voices barely left our lips. The quiet between us stretched long, heavy with worry neither of us dared to say out loud.

Out of options and out of hope, we drove to the hospital. Not because we expected to find him there, but because we *needed* to find him *not* there. We needed someone at the front desk to smile and shake their head, and send us on our way with relief.

But as we pulled into the lot, we saw our coach already standing outside. His eyes told us what his mouth didn't. "I don't know anything yet," he said quietly. "Go home. I'll call you."

Go home? *Home*? Sleep? *How*?

Instead, we drove in circles. Through red lights and quiet streets, no destination in mind. We ended up parked outside a Wegmans, sitting in the silence, refreshing Twitter and news sites as if they held the answers our world lacked. Every minute that passed dragged us deeper into a void. It was like the night itself was holding its breath.

And then they came. The headlines. The texts. The calls.

Three of our teammates. Our brothers. Gone. Shot and killed. Mike was alive, but wounded. Fighting for his life.

The ground tilted. My thoughts fell out of order. Grief doesn't always arrive with sobs. It sometimes enters as silence, as breathlessness, as a kind of internal collapse. That night, it was all of that. My heart cracked open, but I hadn't even begun to understand why.

And then came the final blow. The detail that twisted the knife deeper. The shooter, the one who pulled the trigger, was my first-year roommate.

I had shared a room with him when we arrived for summer workouts. Ate meals beside him. Sat in class with him. We had a rhythm. We respected each other's space, swapped small jokes, and coexisted like young men figuring out life.

We weren't best friends, but we were brothers in proximity, in football, in name.

How do you even begin to process that? How do you grieve the loss of people you loved when someone you *once* loved caused that loss?

I felt everything at once. Grief, confusion, rage, betrayal. I stopped sleeping. Stopped eating. My mind played every memory in reverse, searching for signs. A word. A look. A hint. Anything.

But there was nothing. Only silence, pain. A hole that couldn't be filled.

Then came the words from UVA President Jim Ryan, an email sent in the early hours of November 14, 2022:

> *To the University Community,*
>
> *I am writing to provide an update to the various community safety alerts the University has issued over the last several hours.*
>
> *Around 10:30 p.m. last night, there was a shooting on Grounds. One of our students, Christopher Darnell Jones Jr., is suspected to have committed the shooting. The suspect remains at large and is considered armed and dangerous. Multiple law enforcement agencies are coordinating to find and apprehend him. He was last seen wearing a burgundy jacket, blue jeans, and red shoes, and he may be driving a black SUV with VA license plate number TWX3580. First and foremost, please continue to follow the guidance you receive through the UVA alert system, which is currently to shelter in place.*
>
> *As of this writing, I am heartbroken to report that the shooting has resulted in three fatalities; two additional victims were injured and are receiving medical care. We are working closely with the families of the victims, and we will share additional details as soon as we are able. Our University Police*

Department has joined forces with other law enforcement agencies to apprehend the suspect, and we will keep our community apprised of developments as the situation evolves.

This is a message any leader hopes never to have to send, and I am devastated that this violence has visited the University of Virginia. This is a traumatic incident for everyone in our community, and we have cancelled classes for today (Monday, Nov. 14). At this point only designated essential employees should report to work on Monday (all remote employees should continue to work remotely). If you are unsure of your status, please contact your supervisor.

I am holding the victims, their families, and all members of the University of Virginia community in my heart today, and we will make plans to come together as a community to grieve as soon as the suspect is apprehended.

Sincerely, Jim Ryan[1]

GRIEF WITHOUT WORDS

In the days that followed, football vanished. The game we'd dedicated ourselves to, everything we had worked for, became a distant echo. Swallowed by a silence far heavier than any stadium roar. The season was canceled. Practice stopped. Nothing mattered. Each team member struggled to breathe, drowning silently in his own grief and confusion. No words could hold the weight of what we carried. Words felt too small, too fragile to touch the rawness inside.

When we finally gathered for the team meeting, the air was thick. Thick with sorrow, disbelief, and unspoken questions. Coach Elliott stood before us, but he didn't deliver a speech. There were no easy platitudes, no rehearsed lines to mend broken hearts. Instead, he spoke simply: "There is a way forward, but the only way to get there is by loving each other through it."

What followed wasn't a meeting. It was a moment suspended in time. For thirty, maybe forty minutes, we held each other, crying, hugging, sharing pain and silence without needing to fill the space with words. Coach Elliott was there. So were Carla Williams, UVA Athletic Director, and Vince Croce, UVA Chaplain and head of Fellowship of Christian Athletes. They didn't try to fix us. They just stood with us, offering presence, comfort, and quiet strength. In that raw, fragile moment, we finally knew we weren't alone.

Later that day, a few of us drifted back to the facility. Not to train or strategize, but simply to be. To sit in the place that had always held us together, a silent sanctuary amidst the chaos. Sometimes healing doesn't start with speech. It starts with shared presence, even in the quietest stillness.

That week, we laid to rest three young men. Our teammates, our brothers. Young men who had shared our locker room, our meals, our laughter, our dreams. Three mothers kissed their sons goodbye for the last time.

That image, the unbearable, gut-wrenching image of a mother laying her child to rest, is seared into my soul. It breaks something inside you. It makes everything else, like the yards gained, the wins celebrated, and the trophies earned, feel painfully small, fleeting, and fragile in the face of such loss.

Even now, there are no easy answers, just this truth: life changed that night. And we are all still learning how to live with what was taken.

These are the men who lost their lives, my brothers who continue to live in my heart.

D'SEAN PERRY: THE SOUL OF THE TEAM

D'Sean was a true Renaissance man. He could do it all: play instruments, write poetry, make jewelry, and rap. Creativity just poured out of him. He used to send me songs all the time, always putting me on to something new, something meaningful.

He wasn't loud or flashy. He was soft-spoken, but when he spoke, you listened. His words carried weight. He believed in me and encouraged me to keep pushing forward on my own artistic path. That kind of support mattered. It still does.

The last song he ever recommended to me was "Johnny P's Caddy" by J. Cole and Benny the Butcher. I listen to it every day now. Not just because it's a great track, but because it reminds me of him. His taste. His soul. His spirit. D'Sean wasn't just talented, he was inspiring. And everything he touched, including me, he left better than he found it.

At a press conference in Coral Gables, Florida, on November 16, 2022, D'Sean's parents, Sean and Happy Perry, released this heartfelt statement: "Our family is devastated by the passing of our son, D'Sean Perry. He was a loving, giving, caring, God-fearing young man who was full of life and potential… His positive impact was not only felt by our family, but also by the several communities that genuinely loved D'Sean."[2]

LAVEL DAVIS JR.: THE GENTLE LIGHT

Lavel. The first word that comes to mind is smile. He had a light about him. Something warm, something steady. He was always lifting people up, always encouraging.

Honestly, he was one of the first people who truly believed in me. When I was close to giving up, he kept telling me not to quit. That my time would come if I just kept going. And the way he said it, you believed him.

Lavel had this gift of sensing when something was weighing on you, even if you hadn't said a word. He'd show up, crack a joke, offer a few quiet words, or just sit with you, and somehow, that made things feel lighter.

He was a good teammate but also a special human being. One of those rare souls who made you feel seen, valued, and understood.

DEVIN CHANDLER: THE DANCING HEARTBEAT

Devin was pure energy. Always dancing, always laughing. He lit up every room he walked into. He was the life of the party, the *heartbeat* of everything around him.

You couldn't be near Devin without smiling; his joy was contagious. It didn't matter if he was walking out of class, heading into practice, leaving the weight room, or stepping into the dining hall. He was dancing. Always. Like life had a soundtrack just for him, and he made sure the rest of us could hear it too.

But behind all that laughter was someone with a deep purpose. Devin wanted people to feel seen. He wanted you to know you mattered and had a reason to be here.

You could call him anytime, no questions asked, and he'd be there. No hesitation. That was just who he was: present, loyal, full of life. A friend in the truest sense of the word.

One player, who God brought into my life, tried to save his friends.

MIKE HOLLINS: THE QUIET HERO

God knew exactly what He was doing when He brought Mike and me together. What we share isn't just a friendship, it's a divine appointment. A brotherhood woven into the fabric of our lives long before we ever crossed paths. I believe with every fiber of my being that our souls were carved from the same cloth, moved to the same rhythm, and destined to collide in this lifetime.

When we finally met, something in both of us exhaled like we'd unknowingly been waiting for that moment of reunion. And from that beginning, we felt a connection, a purpose. We sensed that our lives had been threaded with the same mission. A message etched into us by God Himself: one of hope, resilience, and unshakable faith.

Even before we could grasp the full weight of that calling, God did. He knew what was coming. He knew the fires we'd walk through, the battles Mike would face, and the darkness we'd both have to endure. And He knew we'd need each other to make it through. Not just to survive, but to rise.

To me, Mike Hollins is nothing short of a superhero. Not in the comic book sense, but in the most authentic, soul-deep way imaginable. He is a man who has walked through hell with his head held high. A man who has endured unthinkable pain and still chooses to show up with courage, with love, and with a grace that can only be heaven-sent.

There are battles Mike fights that the world will never see. Silent wars in the mind, heart, and spirit. And yet he wears his scars not as something to hide, but as a testimony. As proof that even in suffering, purpose can rise. I admire him more than I can ever truly say, for how he bears what could break most people and how he still leads with compassion.

One of my favorite memories, one that still makes us laugh, is from his first year with the team in 2019. We were down in Florida for the Orange Bowl, and during a team event on Miami Beach, the water looked calm, until it wasn't. Mikey, full of energy and maybe just a little too confident, swam out toward a sandbank. But the current was stronger than expected, and before we knew it, he was caught in the waves, fighting to stay afloat. Thankfully, a teammate spotted him and pulled him out before anything worse could happen.

At the time, we chalked it up to a scare and a story we'd tell later. But in hindsight, that moment was something more. That moment marked the beginning of a pull I felt toward him. A pull to look out for him, to check in, to have his back. I didn't know then just how important that instinct would become. How much he would need someone in his corner. How much I would, too. But God knew.

That moment in the ocean wasn't just a warning; it was a calling. A divine nudge that our lives were being tied together for something much bigger than either of us understood. What began as a shared laugh became a sacred bond, one that has carried us through some of the darkest days imaginable. A bond only heaven could have written.

Mike is my brother. Not by blood, but by spirit, by calling, by divine design. And I thank God every single day that He chose to intertwine our paths. Because I don't just get to witness his strength, I get to walk beside it. I get to call it family. ESPN featured Mike in an article in 2022.[3]

UVA RB Mike Hollins Recounts Deadly Bus Shooting through Mom

When a gunman started shooting passengers on a charter bus returning to the University of Virginia from a class field trip on Sunday night, Cavaliers running back Mike Hollins at first thought it was balloons popping.

Then Hollins saw the alleged gunman, former Virginia walk-on football player Christopher Darnell Jones Jr., and screamed at the driver to stop the bus. Hollins and two other students ran off the bus, but he soon realized no one else was following them.

Hollins, from Baton Rouge, Louisiana, told the two students to keep running, but he went back to the bus to help others, according to his mother, Brenda Hollins.

"His classmates are grateful for him because they said he saved their lives," Brenda Hollins told ESPN on Thursday. "He was the first off the bus and told two of his classmates to run, and he went back.

"He said, 'Mom, I went back. I needed to do something. I was going to beat on the windows because no one else was coming off the bus.' He said, 'I was going to beat on the windows. I was going to go on the bus and tell them to come on, get off.'"

But when Mike reached the first step of the bus, he encountered Jones, who Mike said was pointing a handgun at him. Mike said he turned to run, and Jones shot him in the back.

"The only thing he remembers is he tried to turn, but he saw him lift the gun," Brenda said. "He felt his back get hot, and he ran."

According to Brenda, Mike said he started running toward a parking garage and pulled up his shirt. He saw a bullet protruding from his stomach.

"He got afraid that if he ran too far into the parking garage, no one would find him and he would die," Brenda said.

Mike stopped, and a medical student who was on the bus helped him until emergency personnel arrived.

Hollins might have avoided being shot if he hadn't gone back toward the bus. His mother isn't surprised by his actions that night.

"Didn't surprise me," Brenda said. "It would surprise me if he didn't. That's who Mike is, so it didn't surprise me."

Cavaliers coach Tony Elliott also wasn't surprised to learn of Hollins' bravery.

"It's the character that he possesses," Elliott said. "That act is in you before you ever get to that moment. One of the things we talked about in his program is working towards becoming champion men. We talk about heroes vs. zeroes. And guys who set out to be heroic often fail, but it's the common guy that does what he's supposed to do in those adverse moments that becomes a hero. It's the epitome of who he is.

"He's the kind of young man that cares about everybody else. He had other teammates on the bus, and he was going back for his teammates. One of the things we talk about in this program is love, and what love is and what the highest form of love is. The highest form of love is sacrifice, to lay down your life for somebody else. He reacted exactly how I would anticipate. He thought about his teammates. He didn't care if he put himself back in harm's way, but he was going back to check on his teammates."

Brenda said she has forgiven Jones for what he did.

"I already have," she said. "I had to in order to heal so I can help my son. I mean, I don't have a choice. I have to, and then I have to move on to help my baby."

Mike had emergency surgery Sunday night and another surgery on Tuesday to explore damage to his kidneys and abdomen. Brenda said he has been taken out of intensive care, removed from a ventilator, and walked for the first time on Wednesday.

"He's recovering," Brenda said. "Mentally and physically, he's having a hard time. He doesn't know why everything happened, why he was shot one time, why he is here and not his friends."

Brenda said doctors wanted her to wait until after Mike's second surgery to tell him that Chandler, Davis, and Perry were killed. When Mike was intubated and couldn't talk, he asked about his teammates by writing their names on a dry-erase board.

"We had to tell him that we had no information," Brenda said. "We told him that because of the severity of the situation, it was confidential, and we couldn't get any information. I don't think he believed us. He was throwing his hands up and had this look on his face, and I know he was saying, 'Why? What do you mean?'

"We couldn't tell him because we needed his vitals to stay where they were because he had surgery coming up. They didn't want any complications."

Immediately after Mike came out of recovery from his second surgery, his family delivered the devastating news that his teammates were gone.

"He was waiting," Brenda said. "Right after they removed the ventilator, I heard him say, 'Thanks, doc.' I hadn't heard him talk, so it was just a blessing to hear his voice. As soon as we walked in, that was his question: 'Where is D'Sean?' He knew. My daughter was standing closest to him, and he looked at her. She shook her head. She said, 'He's gone.'

"Mike's cry was so deep it was like coming from his soul. It was like a cry I'd never heard before in my life. It was so deep. His cry was so deep. There was nothing I could do. I can't grab him and pull him to me and hug him because he's hurt. I can't move him. It was like he was alone in that moment. We were there, but he was alone."

Mike Hollins and Perry, a junior from Miami, were especially close. Brenda said her son said, "Mom, I don't know how I'm going to live without him."

"Mike, you're going to live for them," Brenda said she told him. "You're going to live for him."

RUNNING FOR MORE THAN MYSELF

After the shooting, I didn't want to play anymore. The fire that had once burned inside me flickered and dimmed until it felt like it was nearly gone. I didn't care if I ever touched a football again. The weight of loss, the shock, the heartbreak crushed every ounce of desire I had left. What was the point? How could I push forward when so much had been taken?

But then, one by one, my teammates found me. Some came with tears in their eyes, their voices breaking under the weight of grief. Others didn't say a word. They just sat beside me, their presence steady and silent, speaking volumes where words failed. They told me, no—they *insisted*—that I had to come back. That I couldn't give up. That this was no longer about me. I was playing for them.

- For Lavel, whose laughter still echoed in my mind.
- For Devin, whose spirit was fierce even in silence.
- For D'Sean, whose light had been stolen too soon.
- For Mike, who was still fighting, still breathing, still standing. Carrying scars that ran deeper than the eye could see.
- For all of us, shattered but trying to rebuild, trying to piece our lives back together from the wreckage.

They said I owed it to those we lost, and to those who were still here, to lead. To be a beacon when everything felt dark. To carry the torch they had passed, even if it burned my hands.

So I came back. Every rep I took after that wasn't just about reclaiming who I once was. Each sprint, each grueling yard, each ragged breath was about becoming something more. I needed to become someone strong enough to carry their memory forward. To honor them in every snap of the ball, every yard gained, every touchdown scored. Because I wasn't just running for myself anymore. I was running for them.

LIVING WITH LOSS, LEADING WITH LOVE

Life has a cruel way of testing us. Of hurling storms when we least expect them. But nothing, *nothing*, prepares you for the crushing weight of sudden loss. When someone you love, a teammate, a brother, a sister, a friend, a family member, dies without warning, it feels like the ground beneath you splits open. The world tilts off its axis, and the life you once knew becomes unrecognizable.

It's not just sadness; it's a rupture. A soul-deep ache that doesn't dull with time, it just changes shape. Grief isn't something you get over; you learn to carry it. You don't move on. You move *forward*, but forever changed. If you're navigating the loss of someone you held close, I am so sorry. Truly.

When tragedy hits, the first feeling often isn't sadness. You're in shock because the mind can't comprehend the finality of it. Everything feels distant, dreamlike. I remember staring into space, replaying moments, convinced it couldn't be real. That detachment, that eerie numbness, isn't weakness. It's survival. It's the brain doing what it can to protect you from the avalanche of pain waiting behind the door.

In those early days, nothing made sense. My emotions ricocheted from one extreme to the next. I'd go from hollow silence to uncontrollable tears, then to rage, then back to being numb. I questioned myself constantly. Was I grieving *right*? Was I feeling enough? Too much? Should I be handling it better? But the truth is, grief doesn't have a map. There's no perfect script. Some people fall apart. Others go quiet. Some scream at the sky. Some go to work like nothing happened. All of it is okay.

And then the numbness fades and the weight drops. For me, that's when the sorrow became a living thing. I felt everything at once. Deep sadness, yes, but also confusion, guilt, and rage. Why did this happen? How could it? What if I had said more to Chris? Done more? Called him one more time? I was haunted by things left unsaid and undone, grasping for some way to rewrite the past.

Grief is love with nowhere to go. And when it hits, it demands to be felt. There is no shortcut through it. Only the long, painful walk with it, step by step, breath by breath.

GRIEF IS LOVE WITH NOWHERE TO GO.

But in time, you start to carry that grief differently. It becomes part of you. Not a wound that bleeds, but a scar that speaks. A reminder of the love that was real. The bond that was sacred. The loss that reshaped your world. And with that, somehow, slowly, you begin to find your footing again. Not by forgetting. But by remembering and continuing.

CARRYING GRIEF AS A TEAMMATE AND A MAN

For athletes like me, losing a teammate doesn't just hurt. It alters the very essence of what once brought us joy. The field no longer feels like home; it feels like a haunted house, echoing with the laughter, the voices, the presence of those who are no longer there. Every blade of grass, every stretch of turf becomes a reminder, not of victory or hard work, but of absence. Of silence where there should be sound. Of faces you still expect to see but never will again.

I wasn't on the bus the night my teammates were shot. My life was spared. Others weren't. And while I didn't carry the survivor's guilt that some of my brothers bore like a second skin, I watched the question torment them: *Why him and not me?* That unanswerable ache hollowed them out from the inside, robbing them of rest, of peace. It robbed them of the passion they once poured into this game. For some, football lost its meaning entirely. How do you play when the person you lined up next to is now a memory? How do you celebrate when the one you'd celebrate with is gone? The truth is, loss like that doesn't just touch one part of you. It invades every corner of your life.

In families, when someone you love is suddenly taken from you, the loss doesn't just leave a hole; it rearranges everything. Holidays become minefields of memory. Birthdays echo with the sound of who's missing. Even the mundane routines—from the way they buttered their toast to the sound of their laughter from the next room—become sacred reminders of a life that once was. Grief isn't just about missing someone. It's about learning how to live in a world rewritten without your permission.

That kind of grief eats away at your spirit. It wears you down until the simplest things feel impossible. It brings anxiety that tightens your chest, depression that sinks you like a stone, or even post-traumatic stress that replays the worst day of your life on loop. One of the most difficult parts? The isolation.

I remember walking into rooms full of people and still feeling like I was on an island. Friends and family meant well and tried to say the right things to comfort me, but when you're drowning in loss, even the kindest words sound like whispers in a storm. Sometimes grief makes you withdraw or builds walls between you and the rest of the world, especially with those who haven't walked through the same fire. That kind of loneliness is suffocating.

But in the midst of that darkness, there was light. My surviving teammates, our coaches, the University, and really *the entire city of Charlottesville* wrapped their arms around us. They showed up, not with answers or platitudes but with presence. For the rest of my life, I will carry that solidarity, love, and unshakable support with me.

And that's where resilience begins. Not in pretending the pain isn't real, but in choosing to rise anyway. Some of the most powerful acts of strength I've ever witnessed came from people who turned unimaginable grief into purpose: Athletes dedicating every game to the friends they lost. Families creating foundations, scholarships, and movements in their loved one's name. Individuals reshaping their pain into something that heals others.

No, the pain doesn't go away. It never fully leaves. But it *changes*. It softens at the edges. It becomes something you carry not as a burden, but as a legacy. A reminder of love that was real and a life that mattered.

Grieving a loss like this is never a straight line. Some days you'll move forward. Others, you'll fall back. There will be moments of clarity and moments of collapse. But slowly, one breath, one heartbeat at a time, you begin to rebuild. Life is forever changed. *You* are forever changed. But healing, in its own time, in its own way, is possible. And through it all, you learn that grief, for all its weight, is just another expression of love. Of how deeply we cared, and how fiercely we remember.

WE WILL NEVER FORGET THEIR NAMES

Healing is not the absence of pain; it is the quiet decision to keep living while still carrying the weight of what was lost. It doesn't ask you to forget. It doesn't demand that you move on. Instead, it invites you to make space for sorrow, joy, memories, and love. To wake up each day and choose, again and again, to carry their presence with you, not as an anchor, but as a compass.

There was a time when I thought joy and grief couldn't live in the same room. That laughing again meant I was letting go. That moving forward meant I was leaving them behind. But I've come to understand something deeper, something more sacred: *Healing is not a betrayal of the people we've lost. It's a tribute to them.*

To heal is to walk through your grief, not around it. To let yourself cry without shame. To feel the pain without trying to silence it. But also to let the light in when it comes. To smile at a memory, to laugh when something's genuinely funny, to breathe deeply and know you still have life to live.

Grief doesn't go away. It becomes part of you, like a scar, a mark that says: *I loved. They mattered. They are still with me.* You begin to understand that the ache you carry is proof that their lives left fingerprints on your soul. Lavel, D'Sean, and Devin weren't just teammates; they were family. Brothers. Lights in this world that burned bright, and whose warmth remains even in their absence.

Their names still echo in the locker room. Their faces still flash across our memories. Their spirits still show up in the moments we least expect but need the most. And through it all, we learn that honoring them doesn't mean living in the past. It means living in a way that keeps their legacy alive.

So if you're walking through grief, know this: You are not broken. You are becoming. And while the pain of loss may always linger, so too will the love. The memories. The laughter. The impact. Life may never be the same again, but it can still be beautiful.

Lavel Davis Jr., D'Sean Perry, and Devin Chandler, your stories didn't end that night. You live on in every step we take forward, every game we play, every life we touch. You will never be forgotten.

> Lesson 12: God will heal you in times of grief, allowing you to feel peace and joy once again.[IP]

8

WHEN THE LIGHTS WENT OUT

LOCKED IN AND LASER-FOCUSED

Entering my final season, everything in me was locked in: mind, body, spirit. My focus was razor-sharp, honed by years of sacrifice and the quiet, relentless voice in my head that had spoken the same dream since I was a kid: *Make it. Not just for you, but for them.*

I had done everything right. The sunrise lifts. The offseason film study. The extra reps when nobody was watching. I had carved my body into armor and sharpened my mind into steel. And it had paid off. For the second straight year, I had earned the starting role. Not handed, not inherited, earned.

Each week, I took the field with fire in my chest and a calm in my eyes. I held my ground. I delivered. And for the first time in my career, it felt like the game, this unforgiving, all-consuming game, was finally giving something back.

Then came a moment I'll never forget. Late in the season, my position coach (more like a father to me than anything else) pulled me aside after practice. His voice was steady, but his eyes gave him away. There was something deeper there: pride, hope, maybe even fear. He told me NFL teams were calling. They'd seen the film. They liked what they saw. He said, "Finish the season healthy, and you've got a real shot."

In that instant, my heart swelled in a way I can still feel if I close my eyes. It was like every ounce of pain, every setback, every moment I thought about quitting had led to that one breath. For the first time, the dream didn't feel distant. It felt *right in front of me*. I could taste it.

But it wasn't just about me. It was about *us*. My family, who'd carried so much pain for so long. I saw a future where I could lift the weight from my mother's shoulders. Where my siblings could dream even bigger than I had. Where the cycle finally broke.

Then came that first game. I'll never forget it. We lost on the scoreboard, but it was more than a game. It was our resurrection. We were making a statement. We stood tall in the shadow of tragedy and proclaimed to the world we were still here. Still breathing and fighting.

The stadium that night was electric—packed wall to wall with people who needed that moment as much as we did. The crowd roared like thunder, and the air pulsed with something spiritual. When I crossed the goal line and scored, it felt like my soul lifted off the ground. It wasn't just a touchdown. It was a tribute. To Lavel. To D'Sean. To Devin. To the fallen brothers I carried in my heart.

But the battles weren't just on the field. Off the field, I was at war with my own mind. Chris had been my roommate. My boy. I kept asking myself the same questions, over and over, like a broken record: *Should I have seen something? Could I have done more?* The guilt suffocated me. Some days, I couldn't even look in the mirror. Other days, I wasn't sure I had it in me to keep playing.

But I kept going, pushing. Then came the William & Mary game. That day was different. I was locked in. I rushed for over

100 yards. Made key tackles on special teams. But more than stats, it was the way I felt. I was present, grounded, and alive. The fog didn't vanish, but I saw a path through it.

That day, I realized that the weight of grief might never leave, but you can learn how to carry it. You can run with it. Fight with it. Win with it. And when you do, it becomes a part of your strength, not your weakness.

THE PLAY THAT CHANGED EVERYTHING

The following game was on November 9. Almost exactly one year to the day. One year since the bullets and ensuing heartbreak. One year since I lost my brothers and found myself pulled back into the game by pain rather than purpose. Even now, looking back at this time in my life makes me think of what the Bible says in John 13:7: "Jesus replied, 'You do not realize now what I am doing, but later you will understand.'"

We were playing Louisville in Kentucky. The air was sharp, the lights glaring, the crowd relentless. The opening was sluggish, but the energy began to tilt in our favor. I could feel it. We were starting to click.

I jogged onto the field, steady and centered. My heart wasn't racing. I wasn't anxious. I was present. Calm and locked in. Then the call came: a swing pass. Simple. Routine. Muscle memory. I'd run that play so many times it was stitched into my instincts. I flared out, caught the ball cleanly, tucked it tight, and turned upfield.

Two defenders converged. I didn't think. I just reacted. Dropped the shoulder. Lowered the boom. Drove through the contact like I always had. Like I'd done since I was a kid.

But this time, something was different. When the hit landed, time didn't just slow. It *stopped*. It was like someone had unplugged me from the world. My body went dark. Not pain, but *absence.* I couldn't feel my legs. Couldn't feel the turf beneath me. Couldn't even feel my own presence inside my body. It was like I was floating just outside myself, watching the moment from a distance I couldn't explain.

The sky above was painfully bright, like someone had turned the volume up on the light. My chest tightened. My thoughts scattered. But one rose above the rest: *What's happening?* Then panic came, fast and brutal. *Am I paralyzed? Will I ever get up? Is this how it ends?*

I thought of my family. My mom's prayers. My siblings' hopes. The thousands of hours, the surgeries, the grind, the discipline. I thought of how hard I had worked to get here and to *stay* here. And now, flat on my back, staring at a sky that felt a million miles away, the only questions I could ask were: *Why? Why now? Why me?*

I had done everything right. I had walked through fire and kept my faith. I had fought to be a light in the darkness. This wasn't supposed to happen.

And yet, beneath the fear, beneath the confusion, I felt a stillness. A holy silence. The noise inside me had finally quieted. I closed my eyes. I didn't plead. Didn't bargain. Just surrendered. "God, I'm listening. Whatever You want to do with my life, do it."

And in that moment, something shifted in my spirit. The terror didn't disappear; the questions didn't vanish. But I wasn't the same. Somewhere in the stillness, I had crossed a line.

When I opened my eyes again, I was changed. No longer broken or beaten, but transformed. I turned to Ashley Murray, our trainer, my voice trembling, and asked, "Am I paralyzed?"

EMERGENCY SURGERY AND EMOTIONAL RECKONING

No words are profound enough, no syllables sacred enough, to fully capture the peace that found me in that moment. It wasn't loud or dramatic. It didn't shout over the chaos. It simply arrived. Soft, steady, sure. Like a warm blanket draped over cold shoulders. Like light breaking through storm clouds.

It was as if God Himself had stepped into the chaos, reached into the eye of my storm, placed a hand on my chest, and whispered, "Be still." And I obeyed. In that silence, I wasn't on a football field. I was transported back to a wooden pew in a small church in Virginia. I could smell the faint perfume of old hymnals and hear the rustling of Sunday dresses. My legs swung freely under the seat as I listened to my grandmother's voice echo in memory: "Sometimes God shows things only to certain people because He has a special task for them." And somehow, I knew, in that quiet space between pain and peace, I had just been given mine.

Then the rush began. Flashing lights. Fast wheels. The rush to a hospital bed under brightly lit fluorescents. Clipped voices barking medical terms I didn't understand. I was wheeled through sterile white corridors under flickering lights, strangers moving with urgency all around me. I had no time to process my surroundings. No chance to ask questions. My fear and faith hung in the balance.

Emergency surgery. And when the anesthesia wore off, the pain arrived like a storm without warning: sharp, deep, and unrelenting. The doctors didn't sugarcoat anything. The road ahead would be long. Grueling. Full of uncertainty.

And there I was, alone in a hospital bed, surrounded by machines and beeping monitors, my body suddenly foreign to me. Numb in places that once felt strong, still where I was once unstoppable.

For the first time in my life, I was left with the one person I had spent years outrunning: *myself*.

I had always moved to survive. If I were stressed, I ran until the noise in my head quieted. If angry, I lifted weights until my arms burned. If hurting, I sprinted full-speed into the nearest drill. Pain was always something I could outwork, outlift, outrun. But now, I couldn't run. I couldn't lift, and I couldn't hide.

I had to sit. Sit with the fear. Sit with the silence. Sit with the version of me that had nothing left to prove, nowhere left to go.

And then, above the humming machines, I saw it a quote mounted on the hospital wall: "Courage is not the absence of fear. It is proceeding in the presence of it." And just like that, the questions began to rise. They were quiet, haunting, and honest: Who am I without football? Who am I when everything I built my identity on is gone? Why did I even start playing? What is my purpose now?

I was terrified of learning the answers. But for the first time, I didn't run. I *leaned in*. Because that's what courage demands. Not the absence of fear, but the willingness to face it anyway.

And in that sacred space of brokenness, something profound happened. When I woke up from surgery, both of my parents were there, together. Not separated by the walls that divided their past. Not arguing. Not distant. Together. For the first time in my life, I saw them standing side by side at the foot of my bed. I couldn't lift my arms, but I wept in theirs. I buried my face in their embrace and let go. Let go of the pressure. Let go of the pride. Let go of the years I had spent just trying to hold it all together. In that moment, raw, unfiltered, drenched in love, I felt something deeper than any win, any touchdown, any roaring crowd had ever given me.

That was the moment I understood. This wasn't just about healing bones and nerves. It was about healing my soul, rebuilding from the inside out. About discovering who I was, not when I was running, not when I was achieving, not when the lights were on, but when I was *still*—just me, my God, and the question of why.

THE MIRACULOUS RECOVERY

The doctors told me I'd be in Louisville for months, trapped between white walls and worst-case scenarios. They spoke with certainty, their voices weighed down with medical expertise and grim predictions. But they didn't know *me*.

They didn't know my heart or my will. And those were the two things no injury could ever touch.

They couldn't measure the mornings I had risen before the sun to chase a dream no one else could see. They hadn't witnessed the lonely sprints in the rain, the weight room battles when no one was watching, the sacrifices stitched into every muscle of my body. Pain? I knew pain. But I also knew purpose. And I refused to let this injury be the end of me.

So, I attacked rehab like I had attacked every 4:30 a.m. lift session: head down, heart full, relentless. I turned every movement, no matter how small, into an act of rebellion against doubt. I knew what it meant to suffer. But more importantly, I knew what it meant to *hope*.

Two and a half weeks later, just seventeen days after they told me I wouldn't move for months, I walked out of that hospital on my *own* two feet. Not carried. Not limping. *Walking.* And not just toward recovery, but toward *rebirth.*

Each step declared that I was more than a player with a set of stats or a name on a depth chart. I was a man transformed and refined by fire. I defined myself by what I'd found: perseverance, faith, and a calling bigger than the game.

Perris walking out of the hospital

My healing was a miracle. I believe that with every breath in my lungs. In losing everything I thought I needed, I discovered something deeper.

Football had always been my passion. But it took being brought to my knees to realize that passion wasn't my purpose. My purpose wasn't to be under stadium lights. It was forged in the dark through pain, through surrender, through grace. I was meant to walk through the fire to be broken and *rebuilt.* And now, I live to tell the story.

WHEN PLANS SHATTER, PURPOSE EMERGES

Life, in all its beauty and unpredictability, rarely unfolds the way we plan. We draw maps in our minds. Detailed blueprints of where we're headed, who we'll become, and how long it will take to get there. We craft routines. We set goals and chase dreams with everything we have. But sometimes, in a single moment, or over a slow, creeping tide, our future shifts.

Change comes at you like a sneaker wave you didn't see coming. Sometimes it crashes hard: a career derailed overnight, the death of someone you love, an injury that severs you from what you've built your identity around. Other times, it's subtler. Plans unravel slowly. Perhaps the life you were building veers off course. You wake up one day and realize you're standing in a place you never expected to be. For me, that shift was violent, immediate, and irreversible.

At first, it felt like freefall. Like the foundation I had spent years laying had crumbled beneath me. My mind raced, trying to stitch the pieces back together. Attempting to rewrite reality into something more familiar. But no matter how much I fought the truth, it stood firm: life was no longer what it was, and it would never be again.

That kind of realization is a sucker punch to the soul, knocking the air out of you. But after the grief and anger comes a choice: Do I stay here? Or do I learn to walk this unfamiliar path?

Adjustment is never easy when everything you know gets stripped away. I had to retrain my mind, not just my body. I had to surrender the comfort of the old narrative and lean into the unknown. That meant grieving what I lost, but refusing to let the loss define me.

It's tempting to dwell on the "what could have been." To loop those highlight reels in your head, imagining different outcomes, easier roads. But living in that space only deepens the pain. You can't outrun what *is*. You can only meet it head-on. Acceptance, I learned, isn't about giving up. It's about letting go so you can begin to *build again*.

And in that space of surrender, I began to see clearly. I couldn't control what had happened. But I still had power: Power over how I responded. Power over the choices I made next. Power over the perspective I carried with me. I chose not to focus on what I couldn't change, but on what I could still *create*.

Perspective is everything. At first, my injury felt like a brutal ending. But as the days passed, the pain settled, and the stillness stretched, I began to view it differently. Perhaps it was a pause or redirection. What if the path I thought was my dream was the preparation? What if being torn from what I thought I needed was the only way to reveal what I *honestly* had to give?

I CHOSE NOT TO FOCUS ON WHAT I COULDN'T CHANGE, BUT ON WHAT I COULD STILL *CREATE*.

Life's detours don't always make sense in the moment. But sometimes, the broken road leads you to a more sacred place, somewhere you never would've found had things gone according to plan. A closed door can open your hands. A shattered dream can make space for a calling.[IP]

I'm still walking that path. Still figuring out what it means to live with loss, to carry change, and to write a new chapter with unfamiliar ink. But one thing I know for certain: This journey, though different than I had imagined, is still full of meaning. And maybe, just maybe, it was always meant to be this way.

> Lesson 13: Courage demands that you be willing to face your fear and sit with the stillness to find your purpose.[IP]

9

THE NEW BLUEPRINT

MORE THAN A GAME

Football was never the entirety of my being; it was simply the outlet through which I expressed my discipline, my fire, my drive. It was a language I spoke fluently, a platform I stood on proudly, a rhythm my body moved to for years. But it was never my soul. Lying there in that hospital bed, motionless, disconnected from the body that once moved with purpose and power, I could no longer distract myself with speed or strength. The roar and acclamation of the crowd were gone. The pads, the cleats, the tunnel, the lights, it was all gone.

And in their absence, a question I had outrun for far too long surfaced: Who am I without football? That question didn't whisper. It screamed. It thundered in my chest louder than any stadium ever had. It haunted me in the stillness, clawed at my confidence, and stripped me bare. But in that sacred silence, something unexpected happened.

I heard an answer. Not all at once, but like the slowly lifting of fog at sunrise.

- I am *selfless*—not because I want applause, but because I find joy in seeing others rise. I've never needed a scoreboard to validate the goodness of my heart. I give because it's who I am.
- I am *kind*—not naive, not soft, but rooted in a quiet strength that listens, that sees, that understands pain because I've walked with it.
- I am *humble*—because I've been the one left out, the one doubted, the one forced to prove myself in silence. I know what it means to be invisible, and I never want anyone to feel that way in my presence.
- I am *resilient*—not because I'm invincible, but because I've been broken and still choose to rise. Again and again and again.

None of those truths required a helmet. None needed a jersey. They lived in me long before I ever stepped on a field.

And as I stared up at those plain white ceiling tiles, tubes in my arm, and pain pressing against every edge of my body, that realization washed over me like a wave I didn't see coming. For the first time, I understood: I didn't need the game to know who I was. I didn't need touchdowns or trophies to justify my worth. That truth, simple, clear, liberating, brought a peace that settled deep in my bones.

As rehab began, that peace became my guide. I found myself surrounded by people whose battles made mine look small. Stroke survivors learning to speak again, accident victims relearning how to stand, children clutching walkers with trembling hands. And yet, despite the odds, they gave everything. Every breath. Every ounce of effort. Every tear.

Their efforts moved me. They humbled me and broke me wide open. And in that brokenness, gratitude poured in. Gone was my obsession with image and performance. Something more profound took its place: a hunger to serve, to *matter* beyond the game. I no longer wanted just to win; I wanted to impact others and lift them the way I'd been lifted. To carry more than a football, to carry light, hope, and faith.

I FOUND MY MEANING IN THE ASHES, NOT THE END ZONE.

I believe that God didn't carry me through fire just so I could say I survived it. He brought me through so I could reenter the fire and rescue others still burning. So I could speak to those sitting in their own stillness, wondering whether their lives still hold meaning. It does. Because I found my meaning in the ashes, not the end zone, and I know they will find theirs.

THE BLUEPRINT FOR THE CLIMB

So many people move through this world dimmed. Unaware of their worth, blind to the power humming inside them. I've come to believe that my purpose is to help turn those lights back on. That's what drives me now, every single day. I didn't see it at first. I thought I was fighting for *my* career, *my* reps, *my* future. But somewhere along the way, I realized I was building something bigger than a résumé. I was building a blueprint.

For a long time, I carried shame over not making it to the NFL. That shame sat on my chest like unfinished business, leading me to believe I had failed. Failed my family, failed the promise I made to my mother, failed the kid inside me who dreamed under Friday night lights. But with time (as well as pain and prayer), I saw the truth: Making it to the league was never the point. Proving the climb is possible was the point.

And in that, I didn't fail. I *finished*. I left behind a path others can walk: a formula forged in sweat, rejection, discipline, and a relentless belief in something greater than circumstance. That blueprint stands on four unshakable pillars:

1. VISION

Sight is what your eyes report when you're flat on your back at the bottom. Vision is what your spirit sees when reality lies to you. Sight says, "This is over." Vision whispers, "This is the beginning." When you've been counted out, vision is the future you hold onto until the present catches up.

2. EXTREME SELF-BELIEF

Confidence can crack. Applause fades. Rankings change. There will be days you look in the mirror and don't recognize the face staring back. That's when you need something deeper—conviction. A knowing that outlasts doubt, wind, injury, rumor, and silence. A fire no one else can tend but you.

3. PREPARATION

You can't improvise readiness. If you want to win, you do more than is required, especially when no one's keeping score. Maybe that means sneaking into film rooms, studying plays you were never handed. Perhaps it means showing up the day after being overlooked, again. Preparation is how you stay ready when opportunity finally remembers your name.

4. EXECUTION

When the moment comes, it's too late to become who you needed to be. Execution is faith in your work and keeping faith in the lonely hours. Faith that the struggle was seed, not waste. You step into the fire and perform. Not because you're lucky, but because you're *prepared.*

If you can *see* the vision, *believe* beyond doubt, *prepare* beyond expectation, and *execute* when called, you can change your life. I believe that with my whole heart. That's why my focus now isn't touchdowns or trophies. It's people.

My story isn't about *me* making it to the league. It's about showing *you* that you can reach whatever "league" exists in your own life: business, education, recovery, faith, family. It's about rewriting the script for kids who feel invisible, for athletes who think their value expires when the clock hits zero, for anyone who's ever been told "you're done."

THE VIBE FORMULA[IP]

Vision + Intention + Belief + Execution = Winning Culture

ELEMENT	ENERGY	ENDZONE
Vision	Where	The past can hold you back, but a new future can set you free.
Intention	Why	Before you forge your way, you must fortify your why.
Belief	Who	Success isn't found in charting the perfect course; it's experienced by taking imperfect action.
Execution	How	If you want the plan to work, you must work the plan.

THE GIFT INSIDE ADVERSITY

We pray for smooth paths, but it's the rough ground that grows us. Challenges force adaptation. Pain sharpens problem-solving. Setbacks build internal load-bearing walls you didn't know you needed. Remove the struggle, and most of us would never stretch past average.

My own story would be unrecognizable if:

- My dad hadn't pushed me through drills I hated.
- Coaches hadn't overlooked me until I learned to outwork the room.
- Injury hadn't stripped away the identity I hid behind.

Pressure shaped all of it. This isn't just me. Look around: many people who changed the world were forged in the face of loss, failure, and resistance. Thomas Edison burned through thousands of attempts before the lightbulb finally stayed lit. Oprah Winfrey endured trauma, rejection, and public setbacks long before she became a global force for connection and truth. These aren't anomalies; they're reminders. Adversity refines. It prepares us for opportunities we couldn't have taken earlier.

YOUR TURN

At some time in your life, you've been told to settle. A dream you've downgraded. A part of you that dimmed after disappointment. I'm telling you: that's the ground where vision begins. Ask yourself:

- What do I *see* that isn't visible yet?
- What belief do I need to reclaim?
- Where can I prepare when no one's watching?
- What will execution look like when my moment arrives?

You don't need a stadium to live with purpose. You need willingness. You need honesty. You need the courage to build when the world isn't looking.

YOUR GOAL IS NEVER JUST TO CLIMB; YOUR GOAL IS TO LIFT.

I'm still learning, but I'm still helping others find their power. If my journey gives you a map, take it. Mark it up, make it yours, and then pass it on. Your goal is never just to climb; your goal is to lift.

WHY PERSEVERANCE MATTERS

The doorway to opportunity often stands hidden behind walls of adversity, and the key to unlocking it is *perseverance*. When life throws its weight against you, you're left with two choices: fold or fight. In other words: give in or dig in. The ones who break through aren't always the strongest, the fastest, or the most gifted; they're the ones who *keep going* despite the doubt, fear, and exhaustion clawing at them like hands in the dark.

I wasn't supposed to make it. Not at five foot six. Not in a game built for giants. Coaches overlooked me, evaluators wrote me off, and people who *said* they believed in me still didn't think I had a shot. But I kept showing up. I kept running toward the very thing everyone said I'd never reach. That's the only reason I got the opportunities I did. Not because I was the obvious choice, but because I refused to disappear.

What most people don't realize is this: the moment right before your breakthrough feels almost identical to defeat. That's the moment where most turn around, steps from the summit. Just shy of the clearing. They confuse fatigue for failure and never realize how close they truly were.

The path through adversity is long. It's thankless. It's filled with silence, setbacks, and self-doubt. But for those who keep walking, who press forward when logic says stop, the reward isn't always a trophy. Sometimes, it's discovering a part of yourself you didn't know existed.

Because adversity doesn't just block you. It *builds* you.

Easy seasons keep us safe and comfortable. But hardship forces you to dig deep. When your back is against the wall, or when the plan collapses, and you're standing in the wreckage, you discover what's real. That's when you find strength you never asked for. You find courage you didn't know you had, creativity born from survival, and resilience shaped by necessity. I know this because I've *lived* it.

I didn't ask to be shipped across the country. I didn't ask to face racial isolation, or injury, or to stare down a doctor's eyes as he told me I might never walk again. Those battles were handed to me without permission. But in those moments, when everything felt out of my control, I was forced to find something within myself—my response. My will. And it's the choice to respond with grit instead of retreat that changes everything.

So when the road gets dark, and your legs start to fail, don't mistake that moment for the end. It might just be the threshold. Keep walking your path. Because on the other side of adversity is a successful you, fully formed, refined, and ready.

LOVING THEM WHILE THEY'RE HERE

I know many people who don't have great relationships with their parents due to profound hurts or misunderstandings. And other times, it's just the chaos of life. People grow apart, say things they don't mean, or never learn how to communicate in the first place. When people hear about the bond I still have with my family, even after all the difficulties we've been through, they usually ask, *"How?"*

The honest response? It started with my faith and my grandma.

My grandmother, one of the wisest people I've ever known, had a way of cutting through the noise and speaking right to your heart. She used to tell me, "No matter what happens, baby, you respond with love. That's how you win." Now, I'll admit, when I was younger, I didn't always get it. I mean, how are you supposed to "respond with love" when you're mad, hurt, or feel like nobody's listening?

Young Perris with his grandmother

But over time, her words began to make sense. I started realizing that anger (while normal) isn't what fixes broken things. Throwing gasoline on a fire makes everything burn faster. Yelling back, holding grudges, or staying bitter feels satisfying in the moment, but it never leads to healing. It only builds more walls.

Often, I remind myself that my parents are human. *Just like me. This is their first time doing life too.* They didn't get a magical parent instruction manual when I was born. No secret scroll that told them how to handle every emotion I'd ever have or how to perfectly respond to every challenge we'd face as a family. And you definitely don't get a second chance to raise the same child.

That thought right there helped me a lot. It softened how I viewed them. I mess up too. I've said things I regret, acted out of frustration, and made mistakes that hurt people I care about. So why would I expect my parents to be flawless when I know I'm not?

For a long time, I was confused about certain things from my past. I wondered why we had to struggle so much and why my parents acted the way they did. I used to think that love had to appear a certain way to be real. But now, I understand that sometimes love is simply doing your best when you feel like you have nothing left to give.

I believe that's what my parents did. They did the best they could with what they had. And now, looking back, I can see it. The early mornings. The hard decisions. The quiet sacrifices I was too young to notice at the time. It wasn't always perfect. It wasn't always easy. But it was love.

And, I have to admit, I wasn't a perfect child either. There were moments when I lost my cool. Times I said things that cut deep. I let my anger speak before my heart could catch up. I got defensive and made assumptions. I played the blame game.

But now I understand that relationships aren't about being perfect. They're about choosing grace, giving second chances.

Having the humility to say, "I messed up. I was wrong. I'm sorry."

RELATIONSHIPS AREN'T ABOUT BEING PERFECT. THEY'RE ABOUT CHOOSING GRACE, GIVING SECOND CHANCES.

I've learned something that might be the most important lesson of all: we're all on borrowed time. No one is guaranteed tomorrow. The people you love won't be here forever. So I had to ask myself: "Do I want to spend the time I have holding onto what hurt me? Or holding on to the people who raised me, flaws and all?"

I chose the second option. That doesn't mean I forget the hard times; it means I don't let it define our future. I'd rather spend the rest of my life *loving* my parents than sitting around wishing things had been different. I'd rather call them up and hear their voices than stay silent out of pride. I'd rather hug them while I can than wait until it's too late to say what matters.

Because when you lose someone, it's not the big things you remember most. It's the little ones. The way they laughed. The silly things they said. The moments you rolled your eyes but secretly smiled inside. Those are the memories that stick. And I want to build more of those memories.

When people ask me how my family and I stayed close through everything, I tell them the truth: *I made a choice.* I chose to believe the best in them. I chose to forgive, over and over, even when it was hard. It was a choice to see their hearts, not just their mistakes, and to love while I still have the chance.

And if you're someone who's had a difficult relationship with your parents, I understand. Everyone's story is different. Every hurt has its own shape. But maybe, just maybe, you can find a tiny starting point. Perhaps a conversation or a text.

"Hey, I've been thinking about you." It doesn't have to be perfect. It just has to be honest.

We all carry things we wish had gone differently. But we also have the power to start fresh. We can build something stronger from the broken pieces and become better people. So yes, my family isn't flawless. But it's *real.* And that's what makes it beautiful.

My advice? Love them while they're here. Because one day, you'll be glad you did.

TURNING PAIN INTO PURPOSE

The truth I've come to know, etched into me not by theory but through lived experience, is that every hardship holds a hidden lesson. Adversity knocks on your door to *teach* you. Sometimes it trains you in patience, forcing you to slow down when all you want is momentum. Sometimes it demonstrates gratitude, showing you the value of what you once took for granted. And at times, it teaches determination or wisdom. These are lessons you never asked for, yet they shape the core of who you are becoming.

These aren't things you learn from a textbook. These lessons come only from the fire. And if you endure long enough, the lessons become tools, sharpened to help you recognize, create, and seize the opportunities ahead.

But perhaps the most powerful gift adversity offers is the *ability to lift others,* to turn your pain into someone else's compass. That's what the great leaders, mentors, and changemakers all do. They take what once nearly broke them and repurpose it into light for those still wandering in the dark. What once felt unbearable becomes the foundation of their calling.

And that's what I want to do. I want to help people shift how they see adversity. Not as a brick wall, but as a doorway. A portal into growth, reinvention, and possibility. I want them to realize they can write new chapters from even the most shattered pages.

One of the biggest reasons I've made it through some of the darkest seasons of my life is simple, but sacred: *hope*. Hope kept my lungs moving when life made it hard to breathe. It gave me enough reason to keep believing when everything around me screamed that it was over. See, when pain lingers long enough, it becomes hard to imagine anything beyond it. The tunnel is so long and dark that you forget what light feels like. That's why hope is essential. It is a comfort, but also a *strategy*. It's the fuel that pushes you forward when logic says to stop.

In our darkest hours, hope whispers: *This is not the end.* Just like the seasons turn, winter always gives way to spring. And when we refuse to surrender to despair, we give ourselves the chance to witness that shift or opportunity. Often, the act of *simply believing* that something better is possible unlocks the mindset required to see it when it finally comes.

SO THE NEXT TIME ADVERSITY FINDS YOU (AND IT WILL), REMEMBER: YOUR STORY ISN'T FINISHED. YOU'RE NOT STUCK; YOU'RE JUST BEING *REDIRECTED*.

So the next time adversity finds you (and it will), remember: your story isn't finished. You're not stuck; you're just being *redirected*.

Years ago, I promised my mother, "One day, I'm going to change your life." For so long, I thought that promise hinged on the dream of making it to the league, wearing a jersey with my name on the back and lights above my head.

But now, I see it clearly. I *will* change her life, but not how I once imagined. In a way, far greater. Because the truth is, life doesn't cancel your destination when you take a wrong turn. It just *recalculates*. Reroutes you. It might take longer, the road might twist and rise in ways you didn't expect, but you're still on your way.

So I keep going. Not because the road is easy, but because the story is still unfolding. And I believe, deep in my bones, that the best chapters are still being written.

> Lesson 14: Relationships are about choosing grace over perfection. Be humble enough to admit your mistakes.[IP]

EPILOGUE

People often assume that when the final whistle blows, the story ends. But I've learned that, sometimes, the most important part of the journey begins after the crowd has gone quiet and the lights have dimmed. My story didn't end when I stopped playing football; it simply changed direction.

For a long time, I thought the dream was singular: make it to the league, take care of my family, and inspire people by the way I played the game. And in many ways, I did accomplish pieces of that dream. I earned a starting role. I inspired others. I overcame setbacks. I carried the hopes of a younger version of myself every time I stepped on the field. But when the plans I had for my life fell apart, some things remained untouched. The truly meaningful things, like family, can't be shattered.

Today, I'm deeply grateful for the relationships I've built with each member of my family. It's true that family is forever a part of who you are. And I feel incredibly blessed that my mother, father, and brother not only remain in my life, but continue to shape it in meaningful, lasting ways.

FROM CAREGIVER TO CONFIDANT

My relationship with my mom is one of the most grounding and beautiful parts of my life. She has always been a quiet light in my world. A steady presence who brings warmth and peace, even in the most uncertain moments. No matter how much time passes or how drastically life changes, she remains my anchor.

These days, I do my best to take care of her, just as she spent so many years taking care of me. That role reversal has added a depth to our bond that I could never have imagined as a child. It's no longer just about her guiding me. It's about walking beside each other. That shift has brought a tenderness and a mutual respect that makes our connection even stronger.

Over the years, our relationship has evolved from a traditional parent-child dynamic into something more like friendship. She is, and will always be, my mom. There's no replacing that. But now she relates to me with a gentleness that gives me room to grow. After all we've been through, the highs, the lows, the lessons learned the hard way, she no longer tries to correct or control. Instead, she offers something even more powerful: her presence. Her quiet love. Her reminder that she's always there if I need her.

That kind of love, unconditional and unwavering, means everything to me. Her support is constant. My pursuit of higher education and my dream of building a better future have made her genuinely proud. I see it in her eyes and hear it in her voice. Her belief in me gives me strength on the days I struggle to find it in myself.

She still works at UPS and just marked her seventh year there. But I pray that her time spent in the workforce won't last much longer. She's poured so much of herself into providing and showing up for others, and if anyone deserves rest, it's her.

My mom is more than a parent. She's my safe haven, my reminder of resilience, and the embodiment of quiet strength. I carry her love with me in every step I take, and it continues to guide me as I grow into the person I hope to become.

A LEGACY REWRITTEN

My relationship with my father has always been complicated. Not in a surface-level way, but in the deep, layered, soul-shaping sense. To me, it has often felt heavy, even strange at times, but undeniably formative. As I've shared in this book, our past holds its share of darkness and pain and moments that left scars I'll carry for life. And yet, within that pain lies a surprising kind of beauty. The kind that can only emerge when something broken still manages to birth something whole.

I would not be the man I am today without him. That's a truth I've only come to fully understand with time, reflection, and maturity. The sternness he carried, the discipline he demanded, and even the silence in moments I desperately wished for words, all of it shaped me. The mindset I walk with, the resilience I wear like armor, was forged through trial, pressure, and persistence. It wasn't always easy, and often it wasn't kind, but now I can see that in his own way, he was doing what he thought he had to do. Not just to raise me, but to prepare me. And in that mission, he succeeded.

He remains a crucial figure in my journey, not just for who I've become, but for who I'm still becoming. Today, our relationship looks different. We've both evolved, and so has the dynamic between us. We talk about that sometimes, how the need for his provision has faded, replaced by something deeper: a need for perspective. I don't turn to him for answers the way I once might have as a child. Instead, I seek his wisdom. I ask how to lead, how to carry myself with dignity, how to navigate the more complex corners of adulthood. And like my mother, he gives me space to grow, always steady, always present, always proud.

My father now works for ManTech, a life that looks nothing like the one we once knew. And yet, among all the changes, one of the most powerful shifts has been his pride in me. When I told him I was pursuing my doctorate, his response was unforgettable. It wasn't just joy, it was legacy. He told me this step wasn't just about me. It was about our entire family. That earning the title "Dr." wouldn't just be a personal achievement, it would be a symbol of generational change. That meant everything to him. And it means everything to me.

No matter how difficult our history may have been, I know now, without a doubt, that my father loved me the best way he knew how. And that love, though imperfect, laid the foundation for the strength, drive, and sense of purpose I carry with me today.

TWO PATHS, ONE BOND

My brother and I are, in many ways, a living illustration of nature. Not just in a poetic sense, but in the way that two trees can grow from the same soil and still stretch in different directions toward their own light. We come from the same roots, the same home, the same foundation. We were shaped by the same lessons, the same early storms. But life, time, and personal truth led us down different paths. And yet, neither of us strayed; we simply grew differently. Not better. Not worse. Just as we were meant to.

Our relationship hasn't always been simple. Time, distance, and circumstance created space between us. And finding our way back to each other has been a slow, sometimes awkward process, but a beautiful one. With every conversation, every memory revisited, every present moment we now share, I feel us returning to something that never truly left: our bond. It was always there, waiting for us to notice it again.

He's more than my brother. He's one of my greatest inspirations. There's something about the way he moves through the world, the way he leads with quiet strength and relentless grit, that reminds me who I am and why I keep going. On the days when I feel like giving up, he becomes my mirror, reflecting not just who I am, but who I have the potential to be. He doesn't just encourage me, he believes in me, fully and without hesitation. That kind of belief? It's rare. And it's grounding.

I love him deeply, without condition, without restraint. And I know that love is reflected in the way he supports me, the way he shows up, and the way he celebrates every step I take as if it were his own. He lives in Arcadia, Florida, and wears many professional hats, all of them shaped by intention. He's building something lasting, something that carries his name, his values, his legacy. And I have no doubt he'll succeed. His ambition isn't loud or flashy. It's rooted in purpose and quiet resilience. And I admire it more than he probably knows.

What we share may not always be polished or picture-perfect. But it's real. It's raw. And it's built on a love that has weathered change, distance, and time. I am endlessly proud of him and deeply grateful to walk this life knowing that no matter how far we grow apart, we'll always find a way back to each other.

BEYOND THE GAME, TOWARD THE CALL

I am currently pursuing my PhD in Educational Leadership and Organizational Development. It's a path that may seem worlds apart from the gridiron, but to me, it's just another form of leadership. It's a continuation of the work I started as a player: lifting people up, challenging systems, and making sure the overlooked are finally seen. My ultimate goal is to create a nonprofit that partners with schools, particularly in underserved communities, to offer scholarships and mentorship programs. I want to build a bridge for kids like me, kids who are talented, determined, and full of promise, but mired in environments where dreams often get lost in survival.

I know what it's like to grow up wondering if you'll ever escape your circumstances. I know what it feels like to carry the weight of expectation and disappointment on your shoulders. But I also know what can happen when someone believes in you and helps you believe you're worth the investment.

That's why this next chapter matters to me. I'm not just chasing credentials, I'm learning how to build something that lasts. I want to be prepared, not just passionate. I want to know how to navigate systems, influence policy, and develop programs that actually change lives. And I want to ensure that when a young person is standing at the crossroads, they see a path forward that's paved with opportunity.

This journey has taught me that success isn't about avoiding pain, it's about rising through it. It's about finding purpose on the other side of adversity. I used to think strength was measured in how much weight I could lift or how fast I could run. But now I see that real strength is found in perseverance, integrity, and love. It's in the quiet decision to keep going when everything in you wants to give up. It's in the humility to ask for help, the courage to try again, the faith to believe your life still has value, even when it looks different than you imagined.

Looking back, every obstacle, every setback, every unexpected detour was shaping me. Not just into a better athlete, but into a better man. I didn't understand the anger, heartbreak, and loss at the time. But now I see that those moments were preparing me for this season where I can lead, not from a pedestal, but from experience. A season where I can pour into others with authenticity because I've been there.

I've felt the sting of disappointment. I've questioned my worth. I've wrestled with God.

And yet, I'm still here. More than anything, I hope my story proves that your path doesn't have to be perfect to be powerful. Dreams can evolve. Your life still matters, even if it didn't unfold the way you planned. I hope my experience reminds someone out there that you aren't defined by setbacks. Your response does.

There's something deeply humbling about rebuilding. It forces you to confront your ego, to revisit your why, to dig deeper than accolades. But there's also something sacred about it. Because in the process of rebuilding, you get to choose what really matters. You get to lay a foundation not on hype, but on purpose.

So if you take nothing else from this book, take this: You are not stuck. You are not disqualified. You are not too late. You have a future with your name on it, even if it doesn't look the way you once imagined. You can pivot and rise. You can become more than even your best dreams dared to imagine.

"NOW ALL GLORY TO GOD, WHO IS ABLE, THROUGH HIS MIGHTY POWER AT WORK WITHIN US, TO ACCOMPLISH INFINITELY MORE THAN WE MIGHT ASK OR THINK" (EPHESIANS 3:20, NLT).

I'm still running. Just in a different direction now. And I hope to see you on the path.

"Now all glory to God, who is able, through his mighty power at work within us, to accomplish infinitely more than we might ask or think" (Ephesians 3:20, NLT).

A COACH'S PERSPECTIVE

Perris is an exceptionally humble man who would never seek to exalt himself. Those who know him well, like Coach Tony Elliott, can attest not only to his humility but also to his remarkable talent and relentless drive. Coach Elliott was honored to share his thoughts in response to a few questions, offering a heartfelt glimpse into his deep respect and admiration for Perris.

1. When you first met Perris, what impression did he make on you?

When I took over as head coach at the University of Virginia, I could just tell right away that he had a presence about himself. He was very well-spoken, mannerly, and you could tell he's a genuine person. Then, when I watched him as a football player, what impressed me was how he played a lot bigger than his physical size, and he was willing to do whatever you asked him to do. He was thirsty for coaching. He wanted you to coach and teach him, and he was like a sponge absorbing everything.

2. If you could add something about Perris that you're not going to find in a Google search, what would that be?

He's a man of great depth. He's in tune with himself; he's comfortable in who he is. He embraces all aspects of life, so just a tremendous amount of depth and versatility.

3. Perris talked about his journey as a walk-on and his strategy for how he was able to go from walk-on to being a starter. What made you want to give him a starting position?

He was willing to do whatever, whenever, and do it exactly how you ask him to do it. And then, in fairness to Perris, he's a very talented football player. I think the reason that he was a walk-on to begin with was just because of his stature, not because of his ability, and he just needed somebody to take a chance on him and give him an opportunity. He embraced that, and he didn't shy away from that, and he knew that he had the ability; he just needed an opportunity, and his route to gain that opportunity was through the path of a walk-on.

He also ruled the dice, too, because there's no guarantee that you're going to get that opportunity. But he believed in himself, he was passionate about it, he was determined, and I think it also aligned with who he is. I think, regardless of whether he came in the door as a scholarship guy or began as a walk-on, Perris was, as we say, going to autograph his work with excellence. He was going to be the best version of himself regardless. And we know, as folks who have lived a little bit of life, that that was just God's way of testing him to prepare him for what was to come after football.

4. How would you describe the cultural impact that Perris had on the team both on and off the field?

It goes back to what I said previously. Perris is very comfortable in his own skin. He likes what he likes, and he's not ashamed of that, regardless of what other people may think. He's a team-first kind of guy, and it's not just talk. He lives it. He's going to be about the team. He's going to think about others ahead of himself.

A lot of the cultural things that we wanted to implement as a staff already aligned with a lot of who Perris is as a person and what he wanted to accomplish for the team, so there was a natural connection. But, more importantly, Perris is not afraid to lead, and sometimes to lead, you have to be comfortable being isolated and being alone. And that's what he possesses, because he is very, very comfortable in who he is.

5. In the William and Mary game, Perris had over 100 yards. What did you see when you saw that? What did that say to you about Perris as a football player, and what did you think about Perris's future in football?

It was more of a validation of all the things you saw in the locker room and on the practice field. I had a lot of joy and happiness for him because I know how hard he worked, how much he believed, and how much he sacrificed to have this opportunity. Seeing him succeed is really validation for him and the coaching staff. It bred more confidence. Every time he would have success, it just built more and more confidence for him to continue to fight in that role.

As a starter, you've got guys constantly hunting you down, so there's a target on your back. Guys want your job. They want those meaningful snaps. They want that position of leadership. What was pleasing to see was that when he went from walk-on to starter, he didn't lose his hunger. He didn't become complacent. He just continued to thrive by going back to the basics every single day and relying on what got him there to keep him there.

6. After the shooting tragedy, does anything come to mind about how Perris responded to that and his impact on both you and the team?

He was a guy who was there for his teammates. We were all internally battling with the struggle of processing what happened and figuring out the right mechanisms to function each day. That's tremendously difficult in and of itself, but then to be able to put yourself to the side, to focus on your teammates, and then as close as he was to Mike and to watch him be there every single day, for Mike, was just inspiring to me.

7. So then the following year, that night there in Louisville, when you saw Perris go down and not come up, and saw him taken off the field, and knew it was a significant injury, what was going through your mind at that point in time?

As a former player, and then even as a coach, your greatest fear is that type of injury. And I think, as an athlete, you can grasp all of the other types of injuries; you hurt your knee, you hurt your shoulder, you break a bone. But when you can't move, that's, that that's the worst fear. That walk across the field to get over there to him was a very, very long walk.

And, in typical Perris fashion, he's not even worried about being injured. He's worried about the game. He's thinking about what's going on in the game, wanting to know, did we score? He's really apologetic that he put the ball on the ground. He's in the one place as a football player that you don't ever want to think about. And that's being on the ground, not able to move with an injury that could leave you paralyzed for the rest of your life, and he's trying to apologize for fumbling the football. That's just who Perris is.

In my mind, it's like, "Please, Lord, don't let this be how it has to go. Not for him in particular." Not for anybody, but you don't want this to be the end of the story. And in that moment, we don't know what God's plans are. Human nature is to think about the worst-case scenario. But what we know now is that God had a plan, and it had to go that way for His glory to be shown to the world.

What Perris did after that is remarkable, and it's nothing less than a miracle, but my thoughts were, like, "Please, Lord, don't let this be the way that it has to go. Hopefully it's only a momentary deal. Let Little Mighty Mouse pop up off the ground and go back and finish the game."

8. From that injury until today, what have you seen in Perris?

We see God at work. From where we were on that ground in Louisville to the scenes inside the hospital room and seeing the young man going from not being able to move and questioning if he will ever walk again to now, how he's back lifting weights and looks great, is telling that story. What I've seen is how God can take what we did, what we see as a mess, and turn it into a message.

9. When you think about the future now for Perris, you know, what would be your prayer for him and what you hope God can continue to achieve through his life?

My prayer for Perris is just to learn from the great man in the Bible and be the one who doesn't fall short. God has an unbelievable plan for your life, and what you've already been able to accomplish pales in comparison to what he has in store for you. Stay the course, don't grow weary. Fight every day to continue to walk on His grace and His mercy, and we'll be talking about things that can never be imagined. I mean, Perris could be the President of the United States. Perris could be an astronaut. All of the things that are extremely hard to do, Perris could accomplish them all because you've already seen what he's been able to do. My biggest prayer is that he stays faithful and continues to walk in the light. And as the success comes, to manage it and handle it the right way, and we'll continue to have manuscripts written about his story.[4]

Perris with Coach Elliott

RESOURCES

1. Ryan, Jim. "*To the University Community, I am writing to provide an update to the various community safety alerts the University has issued over the last several hours.*" Email from UVA President. Monday, Nov. 14, 2022, 4:12 AM.
2. WDBJ7 Staff. "Family of UVA shooting victim speaks about gun violence." News conference. November 16, 2022. WDBJ. https://www.wdbj7.com/2022/11/16/family-uva-shooting-victim-speaks-about-gun-violence/?utm_source=chatgpt.com.
3. Schlabach, Mark. "UVS RB Mike Hollins recounts deadly bus shooting through mom." ESPN. November 17, 2022. https://www.espn.com/college-football/story/_/id/35047368/uva-rb-hollins-recounts-virginia-shooting-events-mom.
4. Tony Elliott, online interview with Jonathan Cotten, August 7, 2025.

ACKNOWLEDGMENTS

First and foremost, all glory is given to God, the Most High. None of this would be possible without His grace. This story is not mine alone. It is His story; I am simply the vessel through which he is telling it.

To my parents, Andrea Shine and Stevie Jones Jr., your influence on my life extends far beyond what words can capture. No matter the doubts you may carry, I hope you can look at me with pride and peace, knowing that you gave your all. Your efforts, sacrifices, mistakes, and love shaped me into who I am today.

To my family, in every form that word can hold, thank you. Whether by blood, bond, or circumstance, each of you has played a meaningful role in my journey. From relatives to lifelong friends, from coaches who became father figures to teammates who became brothers, and even to the nurses and doctors who became aunts and uncles, your presence has been instrumental in my growth. I carry each of you with me in this work.

Finally, I extend my sincere gratitude to Jonathan Cotten, Laura Worosher, and Eleonora Cino. Mr. Cotten, thank you for your mentorship and for believing in me enough to open doors that have shaped my path. Laura, your guidance and dedication helped transform this story into something that can be felt, understood, and appreciated. Eleonora, your support, organization, and steady presence have meant more than I can express. You have helped me stay grounded, focused, and prepared every step of the way.

To all who have contributed to this journey, directly or indirectly, thank you. This work stands as a reflection of your impact as much as it does my own.

ABOUT THE AUTHOR

Perris Jones, a former University of Virginia running back, suffered a life-altering spinal cord injury that abruptly ended his career. Refusing to let the injury dictate his future, today, he's a PhD candidate in Educational Leadership and Organizational Development, focusing on creating systems to support young people facing the same challenges.

Perris also serves as a mentor and speaker through Character First Athletics, an organization dedicated to helping college athletes navigate the modern world of NIL (Name, Image, and Likeness) with integrity, purpose, and high character. As an athlete, scholar, and motivator, his mission is to prove that pain can produce purpose—and that no matter how your story begins, it can still end in victory.

Connect at info@characterfirstathletics.com.

FROM PAIN TO PURPOSE:
THE PERRIS JONES STORY

Lessons in Perseverance, Overcoming Adversity, Resilience, Leadership, and Faith

KEYNOTE SPEAKER • AUTHOR • LEADER

BOOK PERRIS FOR YOUR NEXT EVENT

PerrisMJones.com

CONNECT WITH PERRIS JONES

Follow him on your favorite social media platforms today.

@p__m__j

@p__m__j

@iampmj2

PerrisMJones.com

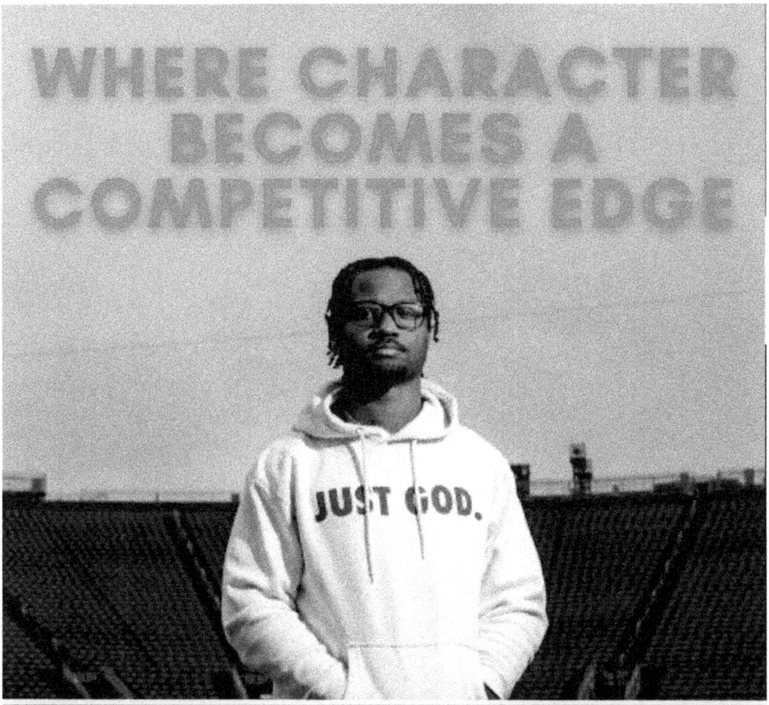

www.ingramcontent.com/pod-product-compliance
Lightning Source LLC
Chambersburg PA
CBHW060433030826
49196CB00029B/251
9781636806129